PERPLEXING PROVERBS

FOR WOMEN

PERPLEXING PROVERBS

FOR WOMEN

A Bible Study by

SUSANNE SCHEPPMANN

Advancing the Ministries of the Gospel
 **AMG** *Publishers*

God's Word to you is our highest calling.

Following God

PERPLEXING PROVERBS FOR WOMEN

© 2007 by Susanne Scheppmann

First Printing, 2007

ISBN 10: 0-89957-247-2
ISBN 13: 978-0-89957-247-5

Cover design by ImageWright Marketing and Design, Chattanooga, TN
Layout by Jennifer Ross and Rick Steele
Editing by Rick Steele

Printed in Canada
11 10 09 08 07 –T– 5 4 3 2 1

This book is dedicated to

Kay Shurtliff,

my mother and mentor in life. You were the person who saw beyond the stringy haired, sullen-faced fourteen-year-old and perceived my potential. You bought my first Smith-Corona typewriter that launched my love for writing. But more importantly, you introduced me to the eternal love of my life, the Lord Jesus Christ. How can I ever thank you?
I love you.
Susanne

Acknowledgments

First and foremost, I want to thank my Lord and Savior, Jesus Christ. The day I met Him, my life changed forever. There are no words to describe my gratitude for His love, patience, and kindness.

Thank you to AMG Publishers, especially Dan Penwell, who never discouraged me in my writing. You will always remain a friend, Dan. Also to Rick Steele, a big THANK YOU, for your patience with editing this study as I learned the "formatting" necessary for publication in the Following God Series.

My appreciation flows to all my friends at Proverbs 31 Ministries whom I serve with day-to-day.

Thank you to The Crossing, my home church. Thank you to my pastors, Shane Philip and Scott Whaley. How I miss working with you guys!

My love to all my girlfriends who have encouraged me in ministry: Connie, Shelley, Teresa, Karen, Sally, Debbie, Sarah, Beth, Lisa, Sharon, Monika, Sue, Margaret, Julie, Sandra, and Mary, your prayers, words of encouragement, and not to mention, your antics helped me to write *Perplexing Proverbs*!

Thank you to Marita Littauer, President of CLASS Services, who taught me the ropes of speaking and writing.

Joanne Sampl only you know the gift you are to me! God placed you and Next-Step-Up Communications in my life at the exact moment I needed your friendship and expertise.

To my children, Jeremy and Stephanie, Darryl and Wendy, and Erin, I love you more than life itself. Thank you for your friendship and the laughter you provide in my life.

Finally to Mark, my husband, what can I say? Without your love and support throughout the years, this book could not have come to fruition. Thank you for allowing me "get-away time." Thank you for serving me tea when I desperately needed a jolt of caffeine to clear writer's block. Thank you, Sweetheart.

 SUSANNE SCHEPPMANN

About the Author

Susanne Scheppmann is a popular coast-to-coast conference and retreat speaker. An accomplished author of several magazine articles, Susanne has also contributed to many book compilations.

Susanne has served as a women's ministry coordinator and Bible study teacher for several years. She currently serves with *Proverbs 31 Ministries,* designed to bring God's peace, perspective, and purpose into women's busy lives through books, devotionals, radio programs, and the *Proverbs 31* magazine.

Susanne and her husband Mark have three adult children and reside in Nevada, where she enjoys reading, cooking, fishing, and traveling. For more information about Susanne and Proverbs 31 Ministries, visit the following Web site:

http://www.susanneonline.com

About the Following God Series

Three authors and fellow ministers, Wayne Barber, Eddie Rasnake, and Rick Shepherd, teamed up in 1998 to write a character-based Bible study for AMG Publishers. Their collaboration developed into the title, *Life Principles from the Old Testament*. Since 1998 these same authors and AMG Publishers have produced six more **character-based** studies—each consisting of twelve lessons geared around a five-day study of a particular Bible personality. In 2004, AMG Publishers launched a series of topical studies called the **Following God™ Christian Living Series**, and this release of *Perplexing Proverbs for Women* by Susanne Scheppmann becomes the fourth title released in this format. Though new studies and authors are being introduced, the interactive study format that readers have come to love remains constant with each new Following God™ release. As new titles and categories are being planned, our focus remains the same: to provide excellent Bible study materials that point people to God's Word in ways that allow them to apply truths to their own lives. More information on this groundbreaking series can be found on the following web page:

www.amgpublishers.com

Preface

Do you feel a little lost in the craziness of this world? Do you need direction? Do you long for wisdom in your day-to-day decisions?

I have great news! Biblical proverbs can help to guide us to make good choices.

A proverb is a pithy little saying that shouts a nugget of truth. These wise sayings within a condensed wordage pack a punch of wisdom easy to learn and memorize. Most children learn bite-sized morsels of wisdom clothed through a proverb. Look back to your childhood for a moment. Do the following proverbs sound familiar to you?

- An apple a day, keeps the doctor away.
- A watched pot never boils.
- A penny saved, is a penny earned.

These proverbs come to us across the years from our ancestors who learned a proverbial lesson and then taught them to younger generations. Usually a proverb is quick and to the point. It flows like a short poem, usually with a two or four-line couplet.

Our God uses biblical proverbs to bestow His wisdom to us. God has placed a pathway of proverbial heart-prints in the Bible to guide us through the maze of life. The Book of Proverbs, especially, brims with pieces of wisdom for us to utilize in our life. These biblical nuggets of wisdom when heeded provide life-changing knowledge and direction.

Perplexing Proverbs delves into the Book of Proverbs and mines ten essential truths for women who desire a life filled with godly wisdom and increased faith. These heart-prints from God's heart encourage us to look beyond our natural instincts and to learn to walk in godly wisdom.

Although the Proverbs are not promises, they do give us guidelines. They are much like the pirates' code that is referred to by Captain Barbossa in the film *Pirates of the Caribbean*. He said, "The code is more of guidelines than actual rules." A proverb is a literary tool that grants us a general truth that can influence a specific situation. Authors Gordon Fee and Douglas Stuart in *How to Read the Bible for All It's Worth* explains, "Proverbs state a wise way to approach certain selected practical goals but do so in terms that cannot be treated like a divine warranty of success. The particular blessings, rewards, and opportunities mentioned in Proverbs are likely to follow if one will pursue the wise courses of action outlined in the poetical, figurative language of the book."

So over the next few weeks, you and I will explore the heart-prints of the Proverbs. We will grab the truth, the wisdom God intends for us, and we will learn how to apply it correctly to our own individual circumstances. We'll discover how the Proverbs pertain to such critical areas as:

- trust in God
- contentment
- friendship
- finances
- parenting/mentoring
- sexual intimacy

We will examine these crucial topics, plus more, to help guide us in our daily decisions. Each lesson begins with a short prayer to prepare our hearts, a daily lesson, a closing proverb to meditate upon and a section to journal your thoughts about each week's lesson. With each week of study, we will gain godly wisdom to equip us to face the day-to-day dilemmas and challenges we face as women in the 21st Century.

Following Christ,

Susanne Scheppmann

Table of Contents

Heart-Print of Wisdom

The greatest good is wisdom.—Augustine[1]

Past mistakes dot the landscape of my memories. Regrets frequently wash over me. These misgivings range from mistakes in marriage, to parenting errors, to poor career choices. Most of my regrets have been caused by poor decisions I've made. Other life-changing gaffes have occurred through my lack of wisdom. Remorse inundates my heart when I recall how often my mistakes were caused by my doubting God's hand in my life. Or even worse, when I outright rebelled against Him. Is there anything you regret? Do you look back at your life and think, *If only I knew then, what I know now?*

Again I ask, "What regrets do you haul in your backpack of memories?"

In addition to remorseful reminiscences, we carry qualms. We fear we will even make more mistakes in our mixed-up todays and our uncertain tomorrows. I have discovered that we can decrease those odds by gaining wisdom. By studying and applying the Word of God in my life, I am making fewer mistakes. My new wiser decisions have also helped to alleviate some of the regrets of my past. God, through His amazing grace and divine will, has allowed me to accomplish several successful "do overs" in my life. I am eternally grateful for this gift from God.

Although it has been one decision at a time followed by steps of obedience, my life began to rearrange itself the day I began to study God's proverbs and apply them to my heart. They have

What regrets do you haul in your backpack of memories?

become heart-prints that have led me to a life of satisfaction and gratitude. The Book of Proverbs launched me on the path to abundant life with few up-start regrets.

Would you like to begin the same journey? Yes? Then let's begin!

My Heart's Cry:

Lord God, as I begin to study Your Proverbs, open my mind and heart. Show me how to take the knowledge in my head and shift it down into my heart. Teach me to apply the concepts of Your truth to my life daily. Amen.

Word Study
PROVERB

The Hebrew equivalent for the English word "proverb" is *mashal,* which means to represent, to be like, or to compare. Proverbs are not promises, but general statements of truth. Consider the proverbs to be general God-given guidelines. They were written down to present pithy, catchy statements for us to remember the precepts of godly living.

THE FEAR FACTOR

It is only the fear of God that can deliver us from the fear of man.
—John Witherspoon[2]

Have you ever eaten an African Cave Dwelling Spider? Probably not. Neither have I. Nor do I have any plans to devour a spider of any type. However recently, on a reality TV show, a darling young blonde woman munched away on these African spiders in an attempt to win a car. She trembled. Tears streamed down her cheeks. She forcefully swallowed four of the strange morsels. One nasty little critter even nipped her lip with its tweezer like claw as I watched in fascinated horror.

Unfortunately, fear can captivate our lives. Sometimes it's a silly fear, like shuddering as we watch someone else doing something we could never do. Some people actually use this type of fear as a source of entertainment.

But what about the fear that creeps into our lives in the wee hours of the night? The kind of terror that engulfs us in anxiety. Maybe we wait anxiously for the doctor's report on our health. Or after we lose a job, we worry about paying the next month's bills. These types of concerns certainly cause apprehension in our lives.

And then there are the times when the waves of fear wash over us and we cannot even define what we fear. We lie awake with anxiety rolling in our stomachs over unnamed or unreasonable fears. We cannot quiet our churning minds.

The good news is phobic fears can change. Thunderstorms once terrified my young son. Now, he loves loud firecrackers. My little boy feared high bridges. Now, he rides the highest and jerkiest roller coasters. He enjoys the thrill of fear when the metal car slides down the extreme heights and races around a tight corner.

At the same time, the athlete in him holds a healthy fear of his basketball coach. If the coach detects laziness in a player or the team, he requires "suicide sprints"—grueling repetitions of running back and forth across the waxed gym floor. My son dreads the punishment, yet reveres his coach.

Fear arrives in various forms; some good, some bad, some fun, and some torturous. All types of fears penetrate our thoughts. Today we will study about a desirable fear, a fear that will enhance our lives.

📖 Read Proverbs 1:1–7.

List the purposes and themes for the Book of Proverbs according to verses 2–4.

When reading these verses, I am left with the feeling that the author of this proverb must be a parent. Actually, it reminds me of my dealings with my own children. Here Solomon extols the virtues and benefits of attaining wisdom and discipline, understanding words of insight, acquiring a disciplined and prudent life, doing what is right, just and fair. Moreover, he advises us to give prudent counsel to the young.

Sometimes I still feel like a child needing guidance. I don't know about you, but I desperately need all of the above. It is no easy task to live a wise and godly life in the workplace and in our homes. God gives us the key to all of the proverbs in 1:7:

> *The fear of the LORD is the beginning of knowledge,*
> *but fools despise wisdom and discipline.*

APPLY Rewrite this verse in your own words.

_____

_____

_____

To fear God seems like a harsh concept in our culture, doesn't it? How would you define the term *fear?*

_____

_____

List three things that you fear.

_____

_____

_____

Now in the margin read *The Amplified Bible* version of Proverbs 1:7. How does this verse describe fear?

_____

_____

My son fears and respects his coach. List three people you revere. Explain why you respect them.

_____

_____

_____

The phrases *fear of the* Lord or *to fear* the Lord can be hard to understand. They are not words intended to make us tremble in our shoes or frightened of what God is going to do. It is a reverence for the Lord. The book, *Hard Sayings of the Bible* explains it as,

> . . . an attitude of both reluctance and adoration that results
> in a willingness to do what God says. The fear of the Lord,

Did You Know?
PROVERBS

Proverbs are general statements of truth, but not promises from God. They represent general guidelines and concepts for godly living. Though the Book of Proverbs is inspired by the Holy Spirit, it should not be read as literal promises, but rather a collection of statements that point us to truth and wisdom.

PROVERBS 1:7

"The reverent and worshipful fear of the Lord is the beginning and the principal part and choice part of knowledge [its starting point and its essence]; but fools despise skillful and godly Wisdom, instruction, and discipline." (Proverbs 1:7; The Amplified Bible)

then, is absolutely necessary if we are even to begin on the right foot in learning, living or worshiping. . . . But with the fear of the Lord there is a foundation for wisdom, discipline, learning and life.[3]

Reverence for God is the first heart-print for beginning a life filled with the capability to make great decisions.

 A second element of fearing the Lord is found in Proverbs 8:13. How does this verse define "to fear the Lord?"

_____

_____

Part of revering and fearing God comes about by hating what He hates. He despises evil behavior, pride, and arrogance. The more a woman fears and respects God, the more she will hate evil and pride. Why do you think this contributes to wisdom?

_____

_____

_____

APPLY Now underline the word below that best describes your attitude toward God.

Terrified   Nervous   Timid   Reverent   Casual   Contempt

 Read Proverbs 9:10 in the margin. What do we gain when we have a reverent fear for God?

_____

_____

_____

If we live lives marked by wisdom, we will not carry as many regrets. Learning to fear the Lord is the *beginning* of wisdom.

Now here is what I adore about the heart of God. He doesn't bark out orders and then wait for us to figure out how to apply them. He instructs us on how to achieve the results He intends. The rest of this week, we will learn how to become more skilled in making wise decisions. We will incorporate His wisdom into our daily lives.

Today's Heart-Print
The fear of the LORD is the beginning of knowledge,
but fools despise wisdom and discipline. (Proverbs 1:7)

 In the space provided on the next page, journal your thoughts on today's studies. Write a prayer asking God to help you understand and apply the wisdom of fearing the Lord.

"Skilled living gets its start in the Fear-of-God, insight into life from knowing a Holy God."

Proverbs 9:10 (The Message)

Lord God,

_____

_____

_____

_____

_____

_____

WISDOM OR FOLLY?

There is only one way to acquire wisdom. But when it comes to making a fool of yourself you have your choice of thousands of different ways.—Unknown[4]

A frail white-haired woman spoke tearfully into the news camera, "I lost my retirement savings, because I believed he was honest. He seemed so nice." This dear lady's money disappeared in a local scam targeted to unsuspecting investors who wanted to "get rich quick." Not only did she not get rich, she came to the brink of bankruptcy. She acted in folly. If only she had sought wise counsel before she purchased the worthless stock, her savings would still be intact.

As I watched the interview, I shook my head. *How foolish! She should have known better.* However, I quickly remembered how many foolish decisions I had made in my life. From credit card calamity, to assorted addictions, to relational ruin, my decisions proved disastrous, also.

Thankfully, the biblical proverbs direct us away from folly to the path of wisdom. Let's study the difference.

📖 Read Proverbs 2:1–12. List God's instruction on how to obtain the benefits of wisdom.

Verse 1

_____

Verse 2

_____

Verse 3

_____

Verse 4

_____

If we follow the advice in verse 2:1–4, then what does verse 5 tell us will happen?

_____

My Heart's Cry:

Oh LORD, help me not to be a foolish woman. Help me desire and seek after wisdom as a precious jewel. Keep me from folly. Teach me to apply Your truth to my life today. Amen.

If we accept His Word, apply our hearts to understand it, pray for insight and seek it as a treasure; then *we will understand the fear of the LORD and find the knowledge of God.* Now that makes me want to shout, Hallelujah!

List the advantages of obtaining wisdom.

Verse 7

_____

_____

Verse 8

_____

_____

Verse 9

_____

_____

Verses 10–11

_____

_____

The benefits of gaining wisdom bring a sense of safety and peace, don't they? God will guard and direct the path of those who obtain godly wisdom. This doesn't mean that life will not erupt with problems. However, it does indicate that God will lift us above the eruptions. Verse 7 reveals that victory will be ours regardless of the battles we face. This thought of wisdom pertaining to safety repeats throughout Proverbs. Let's study this concept further.

📖 Read the following Proverbs and then note what causes trouble and what promotes safety.

Proverbs 28:18

_____

_____

Proverbs 28:26

_____

_____

Proverbs 29:25

_____

_____

In Day One, we saw how biblical wisdom was defined. The terms fool and folly both include in their Hebrew definitions the ideas of silliness, stupidity and people unable to deal with life in a successful and practical way. Fools act with folly. Fools do not understand life's issues. Fools act in rashness. They are no longer alive to the fear of God.[5]

In television sitcoms, usually one bumbling person causes us to laugh. We laugh because we recognize much of his folly in our own lives and others around us. Interestingly, throughout the first nine chapters of Proverbs, *Wisdom* and *Folly* are personified. Each is contrasted as a woman who calls out to us.

📖 In Proverbs 1:20–33 Wisdom calls to us. What does she state in verse 32–33?

_____

Recently, a godly faith-filled friend watched helplessly as her daughter died of a slow, agonizing form of cancer. We might ask, "Where was the promised safety and security?"

When I think of the term *safety*, my human mind thinks "free of trouble and calamity." God's perspective reveals a different idea. When He states, "He whose walk is blameless is kept safe," a closer translation in the original Hebrew is, "He who walks uprightly, will be *preserved*."[6] God did preserve my friend throughout her tragedy. Her testimony today states, "God never failed me. He walked by my side during the darkest moments. Encouragement poured from His Spirit to mine. He kept me safe from losing my mind, my health and my love for Jesus."

We will study this closer in our next week's lesson. For now, let's move on.

📖 Read Proverbs 9. Write Wisdom or Folly next to the following thoughts.

"Let all the simple come."
"She is undisciplined and without knowledge."
"Do not rebuke a mocker or he will hate you."
"If you are wise, your wisdom will reward you."
"Stolen water is sweet."

In my twenties, I thought I knew everything. "Proverbs are like butterflies. Some are caught; some fly away," was a non-biblical proverb I applied to every aspect of the biblical teaching I had been taught in church and Bible college. I rarely sought the Lord for direction in which path I should follow. Not surprisingly, I made some horrendous decisions. My prayers were instructions to God on how I wanted my life to come to pass, instead of a request for His guidance. When my plans failed, I blamed God. I distinctly remember standing in the kitchen, looking up and saying, "Fine! Then you just watch me live my life, my way." My fist-shaking rebellion brought heartache with no end. My poor choices were based on my lack of fear of the Lord. They changed the course not only of my life, but also for several of my loved ones who to this day still pay an emotional price for my arrogance.

However even during my spiritual mutiny, God continued to guide and direct my paths. Read the two verses in the margin.

 What do both of these verses say to you? Do they encourage you? Why?

_____

_____

_____

"In his heart a man plans his course, but the Lord determines his steps."

Proverbs 16:9

" 'For I know the plans I have for you,' declares the Lord, 'plans to prosper you and not to harm you, plans to give you hope and a future.' "

Jeremiah 29:11

These verses encourage me because I know that even when bad things happen or I make a foolish decision, God is in control. He wants the best for me and will direct my path accordingly. Possessing that assurance is invaluable to me.

At one time, I was a foolish woman. I built my life upon very shaky structures such as money, career, education, and clothing. I believed these things would make me happy and prosperous. I bought into the lies of this world. Foolishness prevailed over me. Then the personal tempest of divorce tore through my life, and my world collapsed. The foundation of lies I had built evaporated. If I had pursued God's wisdom, when the storm hit, I would not have suffered many of the losses that I still grieve today. Bible scholar Warren Wiersbe states, "There is a price to pay if you would gain wisdom, but there is a greater price to pay if you don't."

As we close today's study meditate on the terms *wisdom* and *folly*. Then determine to seek after wisdom in your life.

Today's Heart-Print
For wisdom will enter your heart,
and knowledge will be pleasant to your soul.
Discretion will protect you,
and understanding will guard you. (Proverbs 2:10–11)

In the space below, journal your thoughts on today's lesson. Write a prayer asking the Lord God to help you seek after wisdom and spurn folly.

Oh Lord God,

_____

_____

_____

_____

_____

THE VALUE OF WISDOM

The perfection of wisdom, and the end of true philosophy is to proportion our wants to our possessions, our ambitions to our capacities, we will then be a happy and a virtuous people.—Mark Twain[7]

Do you remember the old song titled, "Diamonds Are a Girl's Best Friend"? Well, recently my sister-in-law received a beautiful diamond ring for her anniversary. It sparkles like a star on her hand. She is all smiles. A girl feels special when she sports a sparkling diamond.

However, even expensive trinkets can be lost. The reason her husband bought the new white gem was an ocean wave had stripped her original diamond ring off her hand. It vanished in the sand and surf. The statement "Diamonds are a girl's best friend" might make for a great tune, but Scripture tells us differently. In today's study, we will discover the value of earthly treasures when weighed against wisdom.

I always instruct my family, "If the house is on fire grab the photo albums and my laptop computer." Sometimes I wonder, *If I could contain wisdom in a wooden box and hide it in my closet, would I choose to carry it out of danger if all else I possessed was to be destroyed?* According to Proverbs 4:7, it should be the first thing I seize. What about you? Not counting family or pets, if flames spouted from your home, what would you grab to carry out the door with you?

_____

_____

_____

_____

📖 Read the following verses. Then draw a line to match the verse to the value of what wisdom is compared to in the verse.

Proverbs 8:11   money

Proverbs 16:16   gold and silver

Proverbs 17:16   rubies or any other desire

APPLY On the graph below, circle how much you value jewelry. Underline how much you treasure money and gold.

⬅———————————————————————➡

Not at all   A little   I like it   I love it   I couldn't live without it

My husband sells insurance. When he pitches an insurance policy to a prospective client, he extols its benefits. He informs them of its hidden value. In the same way, God's proverbs exalt the advantages wisdom creates.

📖 Read the following six proverbs and jot down the noted benefits of wisdom.

Proverbs 14:6

_____

_____

Proverbs 19:8

_____

_____

Proverbs 19:11

_____

_____

Proverbs 24:3–4

_____

_____

My Heart's Cry:

Father, open my eyes to what is truly important to me. Remind me that my possessions, no matter how valuable, are only temporary. Allow me to grasp the eternal value of obtaining godly wisdom. Amen.

"Wisdom is supreme; therefore get wisdom. Though it cost all you have, get understanding."

Proverbs 4:7

Proverbs 24:5

_____

_____

Proverbs 24:14

_____

_____

APPLY Do you find the items below advantages of obtaining wisdom? Number the benefits in the order of importance in your life.

_____ Great power   _____ Discernment

_____ Prospers   _____ Future hope (Do you recall Jeremiah 29:11?)

_____ Patience   _____ A home is established and built

I don't know about you, but I had difficulty in numbering the above benefits. They are all important to me. However, I am thankful that when we seek the heart-print of wisdom, all these benefits blend into our lives.

Today's Heart-Print
For wisdom is more precious than rubies
and nothing you desire can compare with her. (Proverbs 8:11)

In the space below, journal your thoughts on today's study. Write a prayer asking God to help you acknowledge and value godly wisdom.

Lord God,

_____

_____

_____

_____

_____

_____

_____

_____

_____

_____

_____

_____

_____

MORE WISE WORDS

He who provides for this life, but takes no care for eternity, is wise for a moment, but a fool forever.—John Tillotson[8]

Albert Einstein was once introduced to the eighteen-month-old son of a young friend. The toddler looked at the physicist's fuzzy flyaway hair and large tortoise shell eyeglasses stuck atop his eccentric expression and immediately began to bawl. "You're the first person for years," Einstein declared, patting the child on the head, "who has told me what you really think of me." Wise old Einstein realized people do not always speak the truth.

Furthermore, our materialistic world lies to us that we need more stuff to make us happy and secure. More money, more beauty, more fame, and more power. The promotion of this deception began early in human history. In fact, Adam and Eve bought into the lie for the need for "more." Do you recall the line the serpent used to tempt Eve? Let's refresh our memory.

📖 Read Genesis 3:2–6. Paraphrase what the serpent asked Eve.

_____

_____

_____

What did Eve believe she would obtain by eating the fruit?

_____

📖 Read Proverbs 2:6 in the margin. Where do we obtain true wisdom?

_____

📖 Read James 1:5 and then fill in the blanks.

"If any of you _____ _____, he should _____ _____, who gives _____ to all without finding fault, and _____ _____ _____ _____ to him."

Do you lack wisdom? Take a moment right now and ask God to give you wisdom for today. Write out your prayer and date it.

_____

_____

_____

_____

_____

_____

_____

_____

My Heart's Cry:

Dear Lord, help me search for Your truth diligently. Help me not to become deceived by what the world tells me is valuable and wise. Remind me that all the knowledge I need can be found in Jesus. In His name, Amen.

"For the Lord gives wisdom, and from his mouth come knowledge and understanding."

Proverbs 2:6

OK, we have seen Eve desiring wisdom and looking for it in the wrong place. Now let's look at what Jesus has to say about choosing wisdom over the alternative, foolishness.

Read Matthew 7:24–29.

In your opinion, what is the gist of the parable that Jesus speaks to the crowd?

_____

_____

_____

Jesus teaches that a wise man or woman listens and obeys God. His parable taught about a familiar subject—the weather. Several years ago, I lived in Japan when a typhoon tore through the island. My house leaked a little water. It shook as the wind howled, but it stood firm because the architect possessed the wisdom to build the house on a firm foundation.

When we build our lives on wisdom from the Word, then our lives will hold up to the storms of life. If we choose to build on foolishness, when times of trouble hit our fascade of wisdom will crash.

Wise souls build their lives on a solid foundation, the truth of God's Word. Now let's view a few more solid truths from the New Testament concerning wisdom. Match the verse with the recorded truth.

Ephesians 1:8	Knowledge of God's will through spiritual wisdom
Ephesians 1:17	Christ will lavish us with all wisdom
Colossians 1:9	We can ask for the Spirit of wisdom and revelation
Colossians 2:3	In Christ is all wisdom and knowledge

According to these verses, where do we find true wisdom?

_____

After my spiritual mutiny, Jesus wooed me back. In my spirit, I sensed Him saying, "Let's begin again. Rebuild your life on a solid foundation. Search for wisdom in Me." I began to dig deep into Scripture and prayed fervently for wisdom. Now my life is secure in Jesus, regardless of what life might bring.

Let's search for wisdom in Jesus Christ, the Living Word.

> ## "God has hidden all the treasures of wisdom and knowledge in Christ."
>
> ## Colossians 2:3 (God's Word)

Today's Heart-Print

If any of you lacks wisdom, he should ask God, who gives generously to all without finding fault, and it will be given to him. (James 1:5)

 In the space provided on the next page, journal your thoughts on today's lesson. Write a prayer asking God to lavish on you the wisdom found in Christ Jesus.

Heavenly Father,

_____

_____

_____

_____

_____

_____

_____

GLORIOUS WISDOM

Men can acquire knowledge but not wisdom. Some of the greatest fools ever known were learned men.—Spanish Proverb[9]

As a teenager, I remember thinking my parents did not know what they were talking about when they instructed me on life-changing decisions. I didn't heed their advice and chose to do most things the hard way. Subsequently, I attended college as an older adult (not the way my parents recommended). I worked full-time in my husband's office, mothered two active boys and attended university classes. After several years, I eventually graduated with two degrees. I held in my hand the world's version of wisdom.

Yet even then, I wasn't wise. Not until I heeded God's advice did I begin to trust in God's grace to protect me from folly.

APPLY As we close this week's lesson on wisdom, please read the following verses and then briefly paraphrase what each signifies to you in your own personal search for wisdom.

Proverbs 14:8a

_____

_____

Proverbs 17:24a

_____

_____

Proverbs 19:8

_____

_____

Proverbs 23:23

_____

_____

My Heart's Cry:

Lord God, I learned much about godly wisdom this week. Grant me the ability of recall so I may apply it to my daily life. And when I consider myself lacking wisdom, help me to recall Your promise to grant me wisdom, if I just ask. I thank You for Your generosity. In Jesus' Name, Amen.

Sometimes I have the "I wants." I believe I "need" things I set my eyes upon as I watch TV commercials, go shopping, or covet what others possess. Do you have the "I wants"? Many times my prayers sound more like a wish list to a genie in a bottle than to the Almighty God of all creation. Do you struggle with the same problem? From the list below, number in order of importance what you would like to add to your life.

_____ Savings Account   _____ Beauty   _____ Wisdom
_____ Big House   _____ Nice Car   _____ Fame

📖 The author of Proverbs, King Solomon, actually did get to pick what he wanted most in life. Let's take a moment to read about this account found in 2 Chronicles 1:7–12. Then answer the following questions:

What did God say to Solomon? (verse 7)

_____
_____

How did Solomon respond? (verses 8–10)

_____
_____
_____

📖 Do you remember James 1:5 from yesterday? Review it in the margin. Explain how James 1:5 applies to this passage concerning Solomon.

_____
_____
_____
_____

How did God act in response to Solomon's request? (verses 11–12)

_____
_____
_____

I believe the following statement defines the type of wisdom Solomon acquired:

> The word "wisdom" means seeing and knowing the truth. It is seeing and knowing what to do. It grasps the great truths of life. It sees the answers to the problems of life and death, God and man, time and eternity, good and evil—the deep things of God and of the universe.[10]

That is true wisdom.

📖 Read Proverbs 9:12 in the margin. How does this verse apply to the story of Solomon?

_____
_____
_____

Margin quotes

"If any of you lacks wisdom, he should ask God, who gives generously to all without finding fault, and it will be given to him."

James 1:5

"If you are wise, your wisdom will reward you; if you are a mocker, you alone will suffer."

Proverbs 9:12

📖 As noted, Solomon wrote most of the Proverbs. Read Proverbs 4:7–9 from *The Message*, which you will find in the margin. Explain why he writes, "She'll make your life glorious."

I eventually realized that obtaining two college degrees didn't make me wise. Only when I sought God for His advice did I begin to find wisdom in all areas of my life. *The Message Commentary*, written by Eugene Peterson, states it best.

> Wisdom is the art of living skillfully in whatever actual conditions we find ourselves. It has virtually nothing to do with information as such, with knowledge as such. A college degree is no certification of wisdom—nor is it primarily concerned with keeping us out of moral mud puddles, although it does have a profound moral effect upon us.

> Wisdom has to do with becoming skillful in honoring our parents and raising our children, handling our money and conducting our sexual lives, going to work and exercising leadership, using words well and treating friends kindly, eating healthily, cultivating emotions within ourselves and attitudes toward others that make for peace. Threaded through all these items is the insistence that the way we think of and respond to God is the most practical thing we do. In matters of everyday practicality, nothing, absolutely nothing, takes precedence over God.[11]

I shout a hearty, "Amen!" Do you agree? I hope so, because over the next few weeks we will be studying topics of "everyday" practicality. We have set *wisdom* as the cornerstone. In Lesson 2, we will lay a solid foundation of *trust*. With *wisdom* and *trust* in place, we will then explore the proverbs for advice on various topics including: relationships, finances, friendships, and even on our feminine sexuality.

I am thankful I have finally absorbed the necessity of storing godly wisdom in my heart. God and His infinite wisdom now hold my hand and guide me as I navigate through the maze of life. I challenge you to search after *wisdom*. In closing, take a few moments to journal your thoughts on the following page, *Your Heart's Impression*.

Today's Heart-Print
Above all and before all, do this: Get Wisdom!
Write this at the top of your list: Get Understanding!
Throw your arms around her—believe me, you won't regret it;
never let her go—she'll make your life glorious.
She'll garland your life with grace,
she'll festoon your days with beauty. (Proverbs 4:7–9 *The Message*)

Your Heart's Impression
Journal your thoughts about:

The wisdom of fearing God

_____

_____

_____

Wisdom's value:

_____

_____

Wisdom's benefits:

_____

_____

How will you begin to fear the Lord and seek wisdom (Proverbs 2:1–4)?

_____

_____

_____

Tell the Lord God what is in your heart after this week's lesson.

Lord God,

_____

_____

_____

_____

_____

_____

1. Frank S. Mead, *12,000 Religious Quotations*, (Grand Rapids, MI: Baker Book House, 1989).

2. Ibid., 145.

3. Walter C. Kaiser, Peter H. Davids, F. F. Bruce and Manfred T. Brauch, *Hard Sayings of the Bible,* in iExalt Bible software. CD-ROM, 1997, iExalt, Inc.

4. E. C. McKenzie, *14,000 Quips & Quotes For Speakers, Writers, Editors, Preachers and Teachers,* (Grand Rapids, MI: Baker Book House, n.d.), 553.

5. Warren Baker, D.R.E. and Eugene Carpenter, Ph.D.; eds. *The Complete WordStudy Dictionary: Old Testament* (Chattanooga, TN: AMG Publishers, 1996). #3684, 3687, 3690, 516–517.

6. Spiros Zodhiates, Th.D., *The Hebrew-Greek Key Study Bible* (Chattanooga, TN: AMG Publishers, 1996), #3828, 1522.

7. http://www.wisdomquotes.com/000858.html

8. Mead, *12,000 Religious Quotations*, 469.

9. http://thinkexist.com/quotation/men_can_acquire_knowledge-but_not_wisdom-some_of/334755.html

10. *The Outline Bible Five Translation,* in iExalt Bible software. CD-ROM, 2000, Alpha-Omega Ministries, Inc., iExalt, Inc.

11. Eugene Peterson, *The Message*, in WORDsearch Bible software. CD-ROM, 2003, WORDsearch Corp.

Heart-Print of Trust

All I have seen teaches me to trust the Creator for all I have not seen. I think we may safely trust a good deal more than we do.
—Ralph Waldo Emerson[1]

od just doesn't care about me. Why has all this happened to me? I can't trust Him."

These words hung in the air as I sat with a close friend. I had no quick retort, no foolproof answer for her. At a loss for comforting words, I hugged her.

Answers do not come easily for someone experiencing multiple pain and tragedies. My friend, Andrea, lost her firstborn four-year-old son to a rare form of leukemia after eighteen grueling months of chemotherapy. Her husband lost his job. Tingling and numbness robbed Andrea of sensation on the left side of her face from a bout with Bell's Palsy. Then Andrea's mother and father were killed in an automobile accident a few months later. All these events occurred within six months of each other.

What could I say? What would you say? Is God trustworthy? Can He be trusted when He doesn't seem to care?

This week we will study the Proverbs and other Scripture to discover the reason to trust an unseen God. We'll find how to depend on the Word of God as a lifeline when hard times shake our faith. We'll answer the question, "Why should I trust Him?" Are you ready? Then come along. We have questions to answer not only for our friends like Andrea, but also for ourselves.

Answers don't come easy for someone experiencing multiple tragedies.

My Heart's Cry:

Lord, help me crawl out of the pothole of doubt. Today as I read Your Word, Write it on my heart so that it may become a ladder of hope when I fall into doubt. Amen.

TRUST IN THE LORD!

"Trust in the Lord with all your heart and lean not on your own understanding; in all your ways acknowledge him, and he will make your paths straight." (Proverbs 3:5–6)

Word Study
TRUST

Trust: "to attach oneself to trust, confide in, feel safe be confident secure; to be careless. Rely on. The folly of relying upon any other type of security is strongly contrasted with depending upon God alone. The type of hope that is a confident expectation, not a constant anxiety."

CRAWLING OUT OF POTHOLES

You may trust the Lord too little, but you can never trust Him too much.—
Anonymous

I have always envied women who found it easy to trust God. For me the act of trusting the heavenly Father has proved difficult at best. My faith journey took a repetitive path when it came to trusting God. I believed; I doubted. I believed; I doubted. I believed; I doubted. I fell repeatedly into the same pothole—lack of trust.

I knew that God could do anything. I believed Him to be a God of miracles. His sovereignty and omnipotence I understood. Memorized Scripture danced through my thoughts concerning the topic of trust. Yes, God could accomplish any action He desired to perform.

Aha! My faith stumbled at the consideration of "He desired to perform." I believed He could, but I doubted that He would.

My earthly father, more times than not, failed me in the area of trust. As an alcoholic, he could not give me the love, nurturing, and material provision that I needed as a young girl. Since I believed that my dad could not be trusted, I assumed falsely that my heavenly Father would not provide me with the desires of my heart as an adult woman.

However as I grew and matured in my faith, God has proved Himself utterly trustworthy. Not once, in my thirty-year history of walking with the Lord Jesus Christ, has He proven Himself untrustworthy.

I can say, without a doubt, that God has made the paths of my life straight even when my understanding stumbled. The security of knowing He is trustworthy encourages me to dig deeper in His Word, so that I can learn to trust His hand in my life. Let's dig deeper into the heart-print of trust.

In the margin read Proverbs 3:5–6. What three things are we advised to do?

_____

_____

_____

The first line, *"Trust in the LORD with all your heart"* encompasses the following two instructions: that we should not lean on our own understanding and that we should acknowledge Him in all our ways. Throughout Scripture, we are instructed over 138 times to trust God. Obviously, since the action of trust is important enough to be repeated that many times we should decipher its exact meaning. Before we proceed further in today's lesson, let's take a closer look at the definition of the word, *trust*. But first, write your own definition of trust.

Trust is:

_____

_____

Now let's look at how God defines trust. The most common Hebrew word translated in the Old Testament as trust is *batach*. Study the Hebrew definition written in the margin. How did your definition match-up with the Hebrew definition of the term, *trust*?

_____

What were the similarities and differences in the two definitions?

_____

_____

APPLY Is there a particular phrase in this definition that you seem to struggle with in your personal relationship of trusting God? If yes, underline the phrase or phrases. Do you know the reason behind the difficulty?

_____

_____

Personally, I have trouble relying on God and not myself. It seems when problems arise in my life, my first tendency is to figure out how to fix it. I want to take charge, instead of asking the Lord for help—although, this strategy is not what Proverbs 3:6 advises.

📖 Please reread Proverbs 3:6. If we trust the Lord, then what does this verse say God will do for us in return?

_____

📖 In contrast, read Proverbs 28:26a. What does a fool trust in?

_____

If you're like me, you have already realized trusting in ourselves is just a big black hole that we constantly have to be pulled out of on a regular basis. Sometimes when we begin to realize that we can't figure it out ourselves, we might jump into a different type of hazardous pothole.

In popular culture today, we often look to celebrities where we hope to find the answers to life. We listen to Oprah espouse self-empowerment. Dr. Phil chides us for lack of self-control. Jerry Springer reduces respect for others to zero in a sullied attempt to enable us to justify our own horrific behaviors.

📖 In the margin read Psalm 146:3–4. What does it tell us about trusting in someone other than the Lord God?

_____

_____

Is there someone other than God in whom you put your confidence and trust? If yes, how could they eventually fail you?

_____

_____

"Don't put your life in the hands of experts who know nothing of life, of salvation life. Mere humans don't have what it takes; when they die, their projects die with them."

Psalm 146:3–4 (The Message)

📖 Read Proverbs 28:25b and 29:25b and then jot down how these verses are similar in their instruction.

_____

_____

_____

We shouldn't trust in ourselves or other people whom we consider as wise. These verses state that it is foolish to trust in anyone other than the Lord God Almighty. Let's consider the benefits of committing ourselves to His sovereignty in our lives.

📖 Read the following verses and then match the statement with the reference.

Psalm 31:5   The LORD is far from the wicked but he hears the prayer of the righteous.

Proverbs 15:29   Commit your way to the LORD; trust in him and he will do this: He will make your righteousness shine like the dawn, the justice of your cause like the noonday sun.

Psalm 37:5–6   Into your hands I commit my spirit; redeem me, O LORD, the God of Truth.

Proverbs 16:3   Commit to the LORD whatever you do; and your plans will succeed.

📖 Please review the Hebrew definition of *trust*. Now with these verses we just matched write what part of the definition of *trust* applies to the verse. (There may be more than one.)

Psalm 31:5

_____

_____

Proverbs 15:29

_____

_____

Psalm 37:5–6

_____

_____

Proverbs 16:3

_____

_____

📖 Now read Proverbs 16:20. How does this verse sum up the benefit of trusting God in our lives?

_____

_____

As you finish today's study, why not allow God to reveal the multitude of blessings that come from learning to trust Him? Take His hand and allow Him to guide you through the potholes of life. Will you memorize today's Heart-Print?

Today's Heart-Print
"Whoever gives heed to instruction prospers, and blessed is he who trusts in the
LORD." (Proverbs 16:20)

Confess to Him your areas of doubt and any difficulties you have in trusting Him. Ask God to help you trust Him more each day as you study this week's lesson.

Oh Lord God Almighty,

_____

_____

_____

_____

_____

ROUTE 66 (PART 1)

The Bible is alive, it speaks to me, it has feet, it runs after me;
it has hands, it lays hold of me.—Martin Luther[4]

I rebelled against God. My fist shook in anger as I turned to walk away in my own selfish pride. But God, in His merciful love, wooed me back. I will never forget that moment.

The jazz music of Knott's Berry Farm echoed across the hot pavement. The smell of fried chicken and sweet funnel cakes taunted my stomach. After a long play-filled day, my family and I browsed through the shops. My head peeked through a door, and my nose detected the musty smell of books. A bookstore!

I ambled in to peruse the shelves. Immediately, I realized it was a Christian bookstore. I hadn't been inside of one in years. I almost headed out, but I hesitated.

"May I help you?" asked a sweet voice.

To my own surprise, I answered, "Huh, yes. Could you show me that Bible, please?"

My Heart's Cry:

Lord, today I need to believe Your Word. Help me to see its truth and life-changing abilities. Give me a gnawing hunger for the Bible. Amen.

Did You Know?

DIVISIONS OF THE BIBLE

OLD TESTAMENT

The Pentateuch (The Law)
    5 books

The History of the Old Testament
    12 books

Wisdom Literature
    5 books

The Old Testament Prophets
    17 books

NEW TESTAMENT

The Gospels
    4 books

The Historical Acts
    1 book

Pauline Letters
    13 books

General Epistles
    8 books

The Revelation
    1 book

She handed me a rose-colored leather Bible. I felt my heart melt inside of me. Suddenly, it seemed like I had come home from a long, tiring journey. After I purchased it, I raced for the car. The rest of my family still shopped, but I sat in a little blue Volkswagen Jetta reconnecting to the Father. A prodigal returned to her Father's waiting arms.

I remember hearing His quiet voice in my spirit. "Let's start over. Use my Word to learn true freedom."

Over the next couple of years, I studied the sixty-six books found in the Bible. I learned how to make wise decisions. Forgiveness flowed to those who had hurt me. I parented my two boys with more patience. My husband gained a more loving and devoted wife. I discovered true freedom in following God's direction in my life.

Those sixty-six books became "a lamp to my feet and a light for my path." As I soaked my heart in the Word of God, my path in life became clearer. God's Word developed into a daily roadmap of direction, which I call my Route 66. In today's lesson, my prayer is that we discover the value of the Bible in our day-to-day lives.

 As we begin, circle the importance of Scripture in your life.

means nothing	hear it on Sunday
too busy to read it	guides and directs

📖 Please read Proverbs 3:1–4. Write down the different instructions given in each verse:

verse 1

_____

verse 2

_____

verse 3

_____

If we follow the instructions given in verses 1–3, what do we gain according to verse 4?

_____

_____

We are not to forget the commandments of God, but to remember them. Oh, how I wish I could wear them around my neck as a reminder. But I can study, memorize, and meditate on them, so they are written on my heart. Have you ever been in a dilemma over something, or perhaps fretted about a circumstance, when all of a sudden a passage of Scripture will pop into your head to direct or comfort you? As we study God's Word, the Lord often uses instant-recall to guide us. He never wastes our effort and time when we absorb His Word. Let's move over to Isaiah for a while.

📖 Read Isaiah 55:11 in the side margin of this page. What does this verse promise us?

_____

_____

This verse speaks volumes to my heart. It is because of the eternal power of God's Word that my life has been changed. Once I realized God's Word always speaks truth to my heart, my ability to trust God increased.

Take a moment and read the following Hebrew definition of the word *accomplish*. Then rewrite in your own words Isaiah 55:11.

_____

_____

The Hebrew word translated *accomplish* in Isaiah 55:11 (*asah*), is a verb, meaning "to do, to make, to accomplish, to complete. This frequently used Hebrew verb conveys the central notion of performing an activity with a distinct purpose, a moral obligation or a goal in view."[5]

If we are to learn to trust God completely, we must listen to Him. The most prominent way God speaks to us is through the Bible. We should read the Word with the expectation of hearing from Him on issues that concern us in our daily lives.

I know when my children just hear me or when they really listen to me. I can see it in their faces, their attitudes, and their actions. When they were younger, and I would be speaking to them, many times their eyes would glaze over. I would say, "Tell me what I just said." Usually, they could repeat the words, but not the actual concept of what the words meant.

📖 Read Proverbs 22:17–19.

Sometimes Scripture makes me laugh. I can just picture the Father looking down and saying that last phrase, "even you, Susanne." I certainly have been a slow learner, but He never gave up on me. Praise God that His Word did not return void.

Think of God as your Father. What might the holy voice of God be saying to you right now concerning how you listen to Him?

God desires that we listen to Him as we would to a wise father figure in our lives. Not just hearing, but also really listening to His advice. He wants us to listen to Him as He guides us through the blessings and difficulties of this life. If we don't listen, we can't begin to trust His instructions.

📖 Read the following proverbs and note why we should listen and act on God's Word to us.

Proverbs 4:1

_____

Proverbs 4:20–22

_____

> "So shall my word be that goeth forth out of my mouth: it shall not return unto me void, but it shall accomplish that which I please, and it shall prosper in the thing whereto I sent it."
>
> Isaiah 55:11 (KJV)

"Pay attention and listen to the sayings of the wise; apply your heart to what I teach, for it is pleasing when you keep them in your heart and have all of them ready on your lips. So that your trust may be in the Lord, I teach you today, even you." (Proverbs 22:17–19)

Proverbs 5:1–2

_____

Proverbs 8:32–33

_____

Proverbs 23:19

_____

 Consider these proverbs and then reread Proverbs 3:5 from yesterday's lesson one more time. How would practical application in these verses aid us in learning to trust God?

_____

_____

Although learning to fully trust the Lord God takes time, I believe that as we gain understanding, keep God's Word deep in our hearts, learn to maintain discretion in our behaviors, we will be able to take a few baby steps toward fully trusting His hand in our lives.

This concept of God's Word impacting our lives is so important, that I don't want us to rush through this topic. So in Day Three, we'll continue with our lesson on *trust* and the Word of God.

Today's Heart-Print
"Pay attention and listen to the sayings of the wise; apply your heart to what I teach, for it is pleasing when you keep them in your heart and have all of them ready on your lips. So that your trust may be in the LORD, I teach you today, even you." (Proverbs 22:17–19)

 Write a prayer, asking God to make His Word genuine to your heart, mind, soul, and will. I pray that God blesses you, as we delve deeper into the trustworthiness of our Lord.

Dear Lord,

_____

_____

_____

Trust

DAY THREE

ROUTE 66 (PART TWO)

Nobody ever outgrows Scripture; the Book widens and deepens with our years.—Charles H. Spurgeon[6]

Right after I became a believer in Jesus Christ at the age of sixteen, I read the entire Bible. I devoured every word not once, but several times. My mother became so concerned she sought counsel from our pastor. He said, "I wouldn't worry about it. It can't hurt her."

The pastor was right; it didn't hurt me. Nevertheless, the voracious reading didn't help me either. You see, I wanted only the head knowledge. I was unaware I should apply the knowledge to my heart and soul. No one taught me that life change should occur when I read the Word of God. I only read it; I did not study and relate it to my walk with God on a daily basis.

It was because of this lack of application that I eventually lost my trust in God, despaired, and strode away from serving Him. But as you read yesterday, in His grace and mercy He drew me back to Him with the Bible. Truly, His Word never returns void and empty!

 Take a moment to reflect on what the famous evangelist, D.L. Moody stated, "The Bible was not given to increase our knowledge, but to change our lives." Can you think of examples from your own life where the Bible not only imparted knowledge, but also changed your life? Note areas of changed behavior, attitudes, and beliefs. If you know the life changing verse, jot the reference or the phrase next to the transformed area.

_____

_____

_____

📖 Read Proverbs 7:1–2 (side margin). This portion of Scripture pictures a father speaking to his son; however, these words apply to us regarding any of God's teachings from Scripture. Max Anders writes of Proverbs 7:1:

In fact the father is issuing commands not just suggestions. The word for "command" is also used for the commands of God, reminding us that the father is transmitting God's standards.[7]

The words "commands," and "teachings" in Proverbs 7:1–2 refer to all of God's commandments or precepts found in Scripture. So, what three things do these verses advise us to do with God's commands?

_____

_____

_____

We are to keep, store up, and guard God's teachings as if they were apples of our eyes. Do you know what the term "apples of our eyes" means? It refers to protecting the pupils of our eyes. Our human bodies are designed to protect this vital part of our eyes. With eyebrows, eyelids, and eyelashes (especially with a good coating of mascara), we protect our vision from intrusion from the tiniest particles. Such efforts of self-protection are reminiscent of how God wants us to protect His Word in our hearts.

From the following list, describe how these activities might help protect what God teaches us.

Bible study

_____

_____

Father, I ask for divine aid in helping me to realize the value of Your Word in my life everyday. Give me the ability to absorb it in the very marrow of my soul. Amen.

GUARD TEACHING

"My son, keep my words and store up my commands within you. Keep my commands and you will live; guard my teachings as the apple of your eye." (Proverbs 7:1–2)

Did you know that the Bible contains 1189 chapters? Those chapters include approximately a staggering 31,103 verses. An amazing amount of knowledge! (Rest assured we will not study all of them during this study.)

"Apple of My Eye" is a modern English phrase taken from the Bible. Two different phrases from Deuteronomy 32:10 and Proverbs 7:2 translate loosely as "the apple of my eye." The Hebrew term for it was "little man" referring to the ability to see oneself when looking into someone else's eye. It refers to the eyeball, with the pupil in the center, called "apple" from its round shape. Because our eyesight is precious and our eyelids automatically shut when danger is near the eye, we use the phrase to imply someone or something is precious.

daily devotions

_____

_____

church attendance

_____

_____

keeping a prayer journal

_____

_____

friendship with other believers

_____

_____

All these activities help us to learn more about God's commandments. For myself, I find that I do some of these items some of the time. Place a check mark by the ones in which you are actively participating and circle the areas where you might need some improvement to help you protect the apple of your eye—God's teachings in your life.

Before we proceed further in the proverbs, I want to peek at some basic teachings of God. These commandments will help us understand more about the proverbs we will study throughout this book. Although, this might be familiar text, pray for God to give us new insight as we read these words.

📖 Read the Ten Commandments found in Exodus 20:2–17. Briefly list the Commandments in the order they are given.

1. _____
2. _____
3. _____
4. _____
5. _____
6. _____
7. _____
8. _____
9. _____
10. _____

📖 Now let's jump back into the book of Proverbs. Glance through each of the following proverbs and then identify it with one or more of the Ten Commandments.

Proverbs 14:2	Proverbs 18:10
Proverbs 22:14	Proverbs 14:30
Proverbs 10:1	Proverbs 23:22
Proverbs 6:16–17	Proverbs 26:2

I believe these precepts are essential because they are given for our good and in our best interest. As we follow God's instructions and lean upon His Spirit's leading, we will make fewer mistakes. After God wooed me back to His living Word and instilled in it my heart, not just my head, His truth made my life more abundant and fulfilling.

I feel it is important for us to look at a couple more verses.

 Carefully read Deuteronomy 32:46 and then fill in the blanks.

"Take to _____ all the _____ I have solemnly declared to you this day, so that you may command your children to obey carefully all the words of this law. They are not just _____ for you—they are _____ _____."

Now read John 1:1–5; 1:14–18. Who is the Word?

_____

APPLY Do you know Jesus as your One and Only?

_____

_____

Let's take a moment to commit or maybe recommit to Jesus Christ right now. Ask Jesus to become your One and Only. Ask Him, to be the Living Word in your life. Close today with this prayer on your heart and lips.

My Jesus,
I take to heart all the words You have declared to me this day, so I may tell my children and we will take care to obey all of Your commands. They are not just idle words for me—they are my life. In Your Precious Name as the One and Only of my life, Amen.

Today's Heart-Print
"Every word of God is flawless; he is a shield to those who take refuge in him."
(Proverbs 30:5)

Don't Worry, Be Happy

"Blessed is the man who is too busy to worry in the daytime and too sleepy at night."—Earl Riney[9]

In the 1980's Bobby McFerin, recorded the hit "Don't Worry, Be Happy." As it shot to the top of the record charts, music critics said it was simple, naïve, and lyrically silly. Today it's one of the most popular ringtones downloaded to cell phones. So why does this song still resonate with us?

The answer to that question is that worry has become epidemic in American culture, especially in women. The National Institute of Mental Health states that about nineteen million American adults suffer from anxiety disorders, with women more likely than men to be literally sick with worry.

Jesus summed up the Ten Commandments in two statements. He said, *"Love the Lord your God with all your passion and prayer and intelligence. This is the most important, the first on any list. But there is a second to set alongside it:'Love others as well as you love yourself.' These two commands are pegs; everything in God's Law and the Prophets hangs from them"* (Matthew 22:37–40 The Message). When you study the Ten Commandments, the first four instruct us on loving God; the next six teach how to love others. Therefore, Jesus condensed all ten commandments into two.

Trust

DAY FOUR

My Heart's Cry:

Father, I know I worry and fret too much. Help me to learn to trust in You. Allow the truth of today's lesson to sink deep into my heart, so that my thoughts do not run wild with fear. In Jesus' Name, Amen.

"If you can't sleep, don't count sheep. Talk to the Shepherd."

We worry about our children, our jobs, money, and almost anything else that we have no control over. Actually, what can't we worry about most days?

I battled worry and anxiety for many years. Instead of trusting God, I chose to rehearse the day's worries endlessly in my mind. (To no avail, I might add.) It always seemed the anxiety struck most often at night when I tried to sleep. I couldn't turn off the frantic thoughts. I heard the phrase once, "Worry does not prevent tomorrow's sorrows, but steal today's strength." How true! Not only did the worrying not fix one thing, the next day exhaustion stalked me because of the lack of a good night's sleep. Worry is an exercise of futility.

Let's take a look at what Scripture says about worry and anxiety and then jot down the advice given to us to help alleviate these trust stealers.

📖 Read Proverbs 3:21–24. Consider each verse carefully. Write how each verse could apply to you.

verse 21

_____

verse 22

_____

verse 23

_____

verse 24

_____

Verse 24 speaks volumes to me. As I said, my fears used to strike me hardest in the darkness of night. I think it does for many women. Just recently, a friend of mine told me, "I can't sleep at night for worry that my sixteen-year-old granddaughter isn't home for the night." This dear grandma and her granddaughter do not even live in the same state. I can only assume she doesn't get much rest. So, let me ask you, how well do you sleep at night?

📖 In your Bible, study Psalm 3:5 and 4:8. How do these two verses relate to Proverbs 3:24?

_____

_____

I saw some bumper sticker theology the other day that sums all three of these verses in succinct manner. It read, "If you can't sleep, don't count sheep. Talk to the Shepherd." I say a hearty, Amen!

Well, let's move past the nighttime worry, to all the things we tend to fret about. Below mark an X to reflect where you are on the anxiety scale.

⟵――――――――――――――――――――――――⟶

What worry?　　A little　　Average amount　　Worry reigns supreme

If you worry, list the top five things you fret about in life.

1. _____
2. _____
3. _____
4. _____
5. _____

📖 What does anxiety do to our hearts according to Proverbs 12:25?

_____

_____

📖 Would you like a kind word to cheer you up? Yes? Read 1 Peter 5:7.

Let us consider 1 Peter 5:7. The Greek word translated "anxiety" in this verse (*merimna*) is a noun that means "anxiety," care that brings disruption to the personality and the mind.[10] Now I know that when I am worrying frantically about something, my personality changes. I become nervous and edgy, which results in my being short-tempered with other people. Does your personality change when you are anxious? If yes, how?

_____

_____

_____

📖 Read Proverbs 17:1. How would this proverb apply to anxiety and our attitudes?

_____

_____

_____

Allow me to give an example of this proverb that I recently witnessed. A friend of mine worried constantly over the details of her son's wedding and honeymoon. She obsessed about the catering service forgetting something as minute as a sprig of parsley. Her thoughts rambled on about what might go wrong such as, "What if it rained during the honeymoon?" Although, she held no control over most of her concerns, she almost allowed worry to ruin the joyous occasion for herself.

Consider this Swedish proverb, "Worry gives a small thing a big shadow." Write what this means to you.

_____

_____

How does it apply to most of our worries?

_____

_____

📖 Let's read what Jesus had to say about our concerns. Read Matthew 6:25–34.

"An anxious heart weighs a man down, but a kind word cheers him up."

Proverbs 12:25

"Cast all your anxiety on him because he cares for you."

1 Peter 5:7

Rewrite verse 6:27 in your own words.

_____

_____

_____

In verse 6:26, God reminds us we are valuable to Him, but then He adds fretting doesn't help us at all. Bishop Fulton Sheen said, "All worry is atheism, because it is a want of trust in God." How would you respond to his statement?

_____

_____

Although, I think "atheism" might be too strong a word, I do think we worry and fret because we don't trust Jesus. As the popular spiritual tune goes, "He's got the whole world in His hands," that includes you and me. Read John 14:1 and then fill in the blanks.

"Do not let your _____ be _____. Trust in _____; _____ also in me."

In the margin read Matthew 6:34. How would John 14:1 influence your thoughts about Matthew 6:34?

_____

_____

OK, so what can we do to rid ourselves of the plague of worry? First, ask God to help you. Read Psalm 139:23 and then whisper it back to God. And then read Philippians 4:6 in your Bible.

Read our final proverb for today, Proverbs 3:25–26. And then rewrite 3:26a and personalize it with your name.

"For the Lord will be _____'s confidence.

Today's Heart-Print
"Do not let your hearts be troubled. Trust in God; trust also in me." (John 14:1)

In today's prayer, take time to cast your cares and anxiety on Jesus. Ask Him to know your anxious thoughts. List your primary concerns and visually place them in His nail-scarred hands.

Dear Jesus,

_____

_____

_____

_____

_____

_____

"Therefore do not worry about tomorrow, for tomorrow will worry about itself. Each day has enough trouble of its own."

Matthew 6:34

"Search me, O God, and know my heart; test me and know my anxious thoughts."

Psalm 139:23

TAKE FLIGHT

Faith by its very nature must be tested and tried.—Oswald Chambers[11]

I trust my spouse. I trust my friends. Healthy human relationships revolve around one key component, trust. Without it, relationships fall into a vortex of negative emotions. Friendships unravel. Marriages dissolve without the foundation of trust to bind them together.

Our relationship with God must be built on the foundation of trust. In order to grow in our Christian faith, we must begin to take baby steps toward fully trusting His sovereignty. I am not sure we ever fully arrive at belief, faith, and trusting God this side of heaven, but I do know it pleases Him for us to continually pursue a deeper faith in Jesus Christ.

Although we doubt and we sometimes fear, God shows up in our lives to our amazement. He does with us, through us, and in us miracles that produce trust. Throughout Scripture, He gives us examples of others in history who illustrate the same principle of faith He wishes to instill in us. Today we are going to examine a scared and doubting Gideon, who found God to be utterly trustworthy.

📖 Let's take a moment to read the story of Gideon in the Book of Judges. Please read Judges 6:1–18 and then answer the following questions?

How did the Midianites impoverish Israel?

_____

_____

Where did Gideon thresh the wheat?

_____

_____

What did the angel of Lord say to Gideon in verse 12?

_____

_____

How did Gideon answer?

_____

_____

How and why did the Lord tell Gideon to save Israel?

_____

_____

Below read Proverbs 30:2–3; 6–6:

> *"[2] I'm more {like} a dumb animal than a human being.*
> *I don't {even} have human understanding.*
> *I don't {even} have human understanding.*

My Heart's Cry:

Father, trust does not come easily to me. Throughout this lesson, embed me with the truth of Your absolute trustworthiness. Proof by proof help me to build-up my ability to trust You in all areas of my life. Amen.

[3] I haven't learned wisdom.
I don't have knowledge of the Holy One.
[5] Every word of God has proven to be true.
He is a shield to those who come to him for protection.
[6] Do not add to his words,
or he will reprimand you, and you will be found to be a liar" (God's Word).

How could each of the following verses be applied to Gideon?

verse 2

_____

_____

verse 3

_____

_____

verse 6

_____

_____

Remember my friend, Andrea, who felt God was unfair and uncaring after all the tragedy that had occurred in her life over a short span of time? She didn't feel she could trust Him. Today, Andrea boasts of the faithfulness of God. She realizes that Jesus never shied away from admitting that terrible things happen to good and bad people. He said, *"He [God] causes his sun to rise on the evil and the good, and sends rain on the righteous and the unrighteous"* (Matthew 5:45). Yet Jesus encourages us to place our trust completely in Him. *"Do not let your hearts be troubled. Trust in God; trust also in me"* (John 14:1).

📖 How would the story of Gideon and Proverbs 30:1–6 apply to Andrea's situation?

_____

_____

_____

APPLY How can you apply Gideon's story to your life?

_____

_____

_____

During the time of crisis, Andrea prayed for God to heal her son. She felt Him question gently, "What if this is My purpose for your life?"

Somehow, God gave her the grace, mercy and strength she needed to survive the season of calamity in her life. Although, Andrea still experiences the grief of her losses, she also sees how God has used the horror of these tragedies to increase faith in their family, but more importantly, many of her loved ones now know the Savior.

📖 Read the following verses and write the assurance given in each verse?

Psalm 27:14

_____

Isaiah 40:31

_____

Isaiah 64:4

_____

Today's Heart-Print

"But those who hope in the Lord will renew their strength. They will soar on wings like eagles; they will run and not grow weary, they will walk and not be faint." (Isaiah 40:31)

I want to fly on the wings of faith. I find great comfort in knowing I can trust the Lord to help me, no matter what the future may hold for me. Shirley Dobson, of Focus on the Family, once said, "The will of God won't take you where the grace of God can't keep you." That thought falls right into line with the proverb we began this week's study with: *"Trust in the LORD with all your heart and lean not on your own understanding; in all your ways acknowledge him, and he will make your paths straight"* (Proverbs 3:5–6).

Will you believe you can trust Jesus in all the details of your life? Please paraphrase Proverbs 3:5–6 into a personalized prayer.

_____

_____

_____

_____

_____

Your Heart's Impression

Journal your thoughts about the wisdom of trusting God.

_____

_____

_____

_____

_____

What is the most difficult thing to trust God for in your life?

_____

_____

_____

_____

Extra Mile
TRUST

With a Bible concordance, research the word "trust."

How will trusting God benefit you?

_____

_____

_____

How will you begin to trust the Lord each day? (Proverbs 3:5–6)

_____

_____

_____

_____

Tell the Lord God what is in your heart after this week's lesson.

Dear Lord,

_____

_____

_____

_____

_____

_____

1. http://www.quotationspage.com/quotes/Ralph_Waldo_Emerson/

2. Frank S. Mead, _12,000 Religious Quotations_ (Grand Rapids, MI: Baker Book House, 1989). 448.

3. Warren Baker & Eugene Carpenter, eds., _The Complete Word Study Dictionary Old Testament_ (Chattanooga, TN: AMG Publishers, 2003) # 6213, 876.

4. Edward K. Rowell & _Leadership Journal, 1001 Quotes, Illustrations, and Humorous Stories for Preachers, Teachers, & Writers_ (Grand Rapids, MI: Baker Books, 1996), 19.

5. Baker & Carpenter, eds., _The Complete Word Study Dictionary Old Testament,_ # 6213, 876.

6. Mead, _12,000 Religious Quotations_, 33.

7. Max Anders, _Holman Old Testament Commentary Proverbs_ (Nashville, TN: Holman Reference, 2005) 60.

8. Matt Keller, _How Many Chapters and Verses are in the Bible_ (Deaf Missions), http://www.deafmissions.com/tally/bkchptrvrs.html.

9. Mead, _12,000 Religious Quotations_, 478.

10. Baker, & Carpenter, eds., _The Complete Word Study Dictionary Old Testament,_ # 982, 128.

11. Oswald, Chambers, James Reimann, ed. _My Utmost for His Highest An Updated Edition in Today's Language,_ (Grand Rapids, MI. Discovery House Publishers, 1992) 10/31.

LESSON THREE

Heart-Print of Contentment

Contentment is a pearl of great price, and whoever procures it at the expense of ten thousands desires makes a wise and a happy purchase.
—John Balguy[1]

Contentment eludes most of us much of the time. We covet what others have in their lives that we don't. It may be beauty, cars, homes, thinness, sex appeal, clothes, money, or a host of other items or qualities we value.

Day after day we hear how inadequate our lives are without all these things. Advertisers coax us with the promise that if we purchase their product then we will be happy and, best of all, others will covet what we have.

Today, as I sat down to write this week's lesson, I felt anxious and irritable. My mind raced on about what would make me happier and more content. My thoughts hip-hopped from weight-loss, more money, a needed vacation, less pressure in my ministry, and maybe a facelift.

Perhaps it's not my face that needs a lift, but my life. I definitely needed a life-lift. Now interestingly, I had just read a whole magazine, pictures included, about Hollywood couple, Brad Pitt and Angelina Jolie. Yes, I devoured the whole silly article. I bought into the lie of this world that my life didn't measure up.

My dysfunctional thinking eventually landed me in bed—depressed. And then, I reminded myself I had a book to write. I went for a long walk around my neighborhood. The sun shone brightly, a breeze blew briskly, the birds chirped, and I felt God's whisper in my spirit, "Now Susanne, what more do you really need?"

Tears sprang to my eyes. I admitted humbly that I need nothing, nothing but a spiritual spanking from the Holy Spirit. I strode home. I listened to a Jennifer Rothschild CD. Jennifer is blind. However, she has complete satisfaction in life. In one song, a phrase struck a chord deep within: "Oh how could I ask for more?"

Oh, Father, forgive me! So, with my chastisement etched in my memory, I offer this week's lesson.

The malady of discontent engulfs our society. Let's investigate why we lost our contentment and more importantly, how we can get it back.

Contentment
DAY ONE

IF ONLY I HAD MORE . . .

Covetousness is simply craving more of what you have enough of already.
—Haddon Robinson[2]

The story goes that a mother of two competitive young sons was whipping up a batch of waffles for their Saturday morning breakfast. As the smell of cooking waffles wafted into the air, sibling rivalry hit. The boys began to argue who would get the first crunchy waffle. Attempting to be the wise mother, she said, "If Jesus were here at the table, He would say, 'Let my brother be served first. I will wait for the next one.' " The older brother turned quickly to his younger brother and said, "You be Jesus!"

We want what we want. Now! If we do not receive immediate gratification discontentment creeps into our lives. Today let's discover how our discontent began.

📖 Please read Genesis 3 and then answer the following questions.

What challenge did the serpent put forth to Eve (verse 1)?

_____

_____

How did the serpent respond to Eve (verses 4–5)?

_____

_____

Why did Eve eat the fruit? (verse 6)

_____

_____

What results took place after Eve and Adam ate the fruit (verses 7–8)?

_____

_____

My Heart's Cry:

Dear God, Please forgive me when I covet what others possess. Remind me to count my blessings each day and to find my contentment in You. Amen.

THE FIRST SIN

"When the woman saw that the fruit of the tree was good for food and pleasing to the eye, and also desirable for gaining wisdom, she took some and ate it. She also gave some to her husband, who was with her, and he ate it." (Genesis 3:6)

The wily serpent challenged Eve's basic belief system. He made her doubt what God had said. Satan promised her knowledge and spawned discontent in her heart. Eve fell for it, or should I say reached for it, and ate the fruit. Then she "generously" shared with her husband. (Notice she ate first, just like the boys with the waffles.) Her discontent changed the whole course of the earth. We inherited her discontent.

Let's examine verse 6 a bit closer. Specifically, I want to examine the word "desirable." A closer examination of the Hebrew word translated "desirable" will increase our understanding of exactly what Eve experienced when she gazed at the forbidden fruit.

> *chamad*: to desire, covet, long for, to be desirable, be costly, precious; to feel delight. The term is part of the Ten Commandments. ("You shall not covet" [Exodus 20:17]).[3]

Surely, we can relate to how she felt. It seems like no matter what we have we still want more. My husband says, "You are such a bag lady!" What he means is, I haven't met a bag or purse that I don't feel I must have. They delight me. My closet holds several bags, but I still desire more.

What is in your life that you just can't seem to get enough of?

Regrettably, Eve didn't just want a purse. She wanted knowledge and to be like God. Her discontent led her to sin.

📖 How would you apply the following proverbs to Eve's story?

Proverbs 3:7

_____

_____

Proverbs 7:2a

_____

_____

Proverbs 15:3

_____

_____

Proverbs 27:20

_____

_____

Eve denied the wisdom and truth of words God spoke to Adam and her. She didn't fear the Lord or shun evil. She didn't guard or keep God's commandments, but believed she could be wise in her own power. Her eyes were not satisfied; by her terrible decision she brought death and destruction into the world.

Satan tempted Eve with the idea of dissatisfaction with her current position in life. She desired more knowledge. Do you think pride might have contributed to her sin?

Extra Mile

TEMPTATION

The Bible presents another case of Satan tempting a person. Read Genesis 4:1–11. What technique did Satan use in both situations? Jot down how the temptations were similar in chapters 3 and 4. Note how Jesus responds to Satan.

"Do not be wise in your own eyes; fear the Lord and shun evil."

Proverbs 3:7

Doctrine

NO ONE TO BLAME BUT OURSELVES

When we sin, our misdeeds are byproducts of a series of thoughts and actions that have developed over time. James 1:13–15 states,

When tempted, no one should say, "God is tempting me." For God cannot be tempted by evil, nor does he tempt anyone; but each one is tempted when, by his own evil desire, he is dragged away and enticed. Then, after desire has conceived, it gives birth to sin; and sin, when it is full-grown, gives birth to death.

Eve initially just looked at the fruit. Satan spoke words of doubt, and then Eve desired the fruit. She looked again and lusted after the forbidden. She took, and then she ate of her volition. Satan can tempt, but he cannot make us sin.

Read Proverbs 11:2 and then fill in the blanks below.

"When _____ comes, then comes _____, but with _____ comes _____."

APPLY I believe Eve's disgrace certainly had a tinge of pride hidden within. But what about you? Can you share a time when you were prideful and then disgrace followed?

_____

_____

_____

Or what about the second part of the verse? Has there been a time when your humility resulted in wisdom?

_____

_____

Sadly I have experienced pride, and then, the disgrace. At one point in time, my religious, self-righteous pride hovered as a cloud around me. I was so straight, I couldn't go around a corner. But then, kerplop! I fell deep into sin. Unhappy with my life, I began to look for contentment in a variety of ways. Instead of going to church, I visited bars. I drank and partied with a girlfriend while a young babysitter watched my children. My marriage eventually fell apart. Shame, disgrace and despair flooded my humbled heart. Yes, Eve and I make quite a pair.

But thankfully, the Lord God sought me out, just as he did with Adam and Eve. After I came humbly back into fellowship with Him, I knew my own lack of contentment could do me in. Humility and wisdom go hand-in-hand. So do pride and discontent.

Today ponder Eve's story. Consider the things you think will bring you fulfillment in life. Ask God to help you see the truth about an object of your affection that gleams so pleasingly and delightfully to your eyes that it has become a distraction in your life.

Today's Heart-Print
"Death and Destruction are never satisfied, and neither are the eyes of man."
(Proverbs 27:20)

Dear Heavenly Father,

_____

_____

_____

_____

_____

_____

_____

_____

PRIDE AND PROVERBS

Pride is the mother hen under which all other sins are hatched.
—C. S. Lewis[4]

Do you remember the movie, *Gone with the Wind*? The long tale based upon Margaret Mitchell's epic novel winds through the relationship of the southern belle Scarlett O'Hara and the roguish Rhett Butler. All throughout the tumultuous romance, both Scarlett and Rhett allow pride to block the paths to contentment in their lives. Scarlett won't let plain Melanie know how much she admires her until Melanie lies on her deathbed. Another primary character, milque-toast Ashley takes pride in Scarlett's love for him while it destroys the contentment in one person after another. Each character's biggest flaw seems to be pride. Frank Kennedy dies uselessly for Scarlett's tainted honor. Because of pride, Prissy lies about her midwife capabilities. Until at last, to Scarlett's horror, Prissy cries out, "Ah doan know nuthin; 'bout bringin' babies."

Without the element of pride the script could have gone like this: Contented Ashley tells Scarlett he loves Melanie; Scarlett, although hurt, admits it is for the best; unabashedly Rhett declares his love for Scarlett, and she humbly accepts his statement as truth; Prissy advises getting a doctor, so Melanie's childbirth produces a robust child and a healthy mother. Following this storyline, all characters are filled with contentment and live happily ever. Pretty boring, huh? The intrigue blows away in the wind without the element of pride and discontent.

For most of us, strife and stress rage in our lives. How much of the turmoil can we contribute to our pride? Today we are going to look at what the Proverbs tells us about the malady of pride and the remedy—humility.

As we begin, please read the quote in the margin. "I define ego as Edging God Out" relates exactly to how pride began. As you read the following verses, please understand they reveal much about Satan and the origin of his evil discontent. Although directed toward the king of Tyre, they also explain the fall of Satan from heaven. The footnote in my Bible explains, "This passage is similar to the one found in Isaiah chapter 14, in that it begins as a prophecy against an earthly ruler but leads into an oracle against Satan, the real power behind the pagan king."[5] The book, *Hard Sayings of the Bible,* agrees with this statement,

> "The historic fall of Satan, otherwise not directly described in the Bible but alluded to in a number of passages, applied the background terminology and metaphor for this text, just as it did for Isaiah 14. His fall from heaven apparently back before time began will supply the model for the fall of the king of Tyre."[6]

📖 OK, let's dig into some Scripture passages that deal with pride. Please read Ezekiel 28:11–19, Isaiah 14:12–15, and Luke 10:18.

Describe in your own words what was the first spark of evil in Satan?

_____

_____

My Heart's Cry:

Lord, reveal my own prideful attitudes to me. Teach me the attitude of humility toward others, but most importantly toward You. In Jesus' name, Amen.

DEFINITION OF EGO

Kenneth Blanchard states in *Servant Leader* his definition of ego. He writes, "I define ego as **E**dging **G**od **O**ut."[x]

"Your heart became proud on account of your beauty, and you corrupted your wisdom because of your splendor."

Ezekiel 28:17

Paraphrase what Satan says in Isaiah 14:13–14.

_____

_____

_____

What was he dissatisfied with in his position?

_____

_____

_____

It seems that all evil begins with pride. Pride initiates discontentment, longs to be the best and desires more. Pride is never satisfied. Do your recall Proverbs 11:2 from yesterday's study of Eve. Let's reread it in the margin, and then read the following Word Study sidebar that adds further insight through explaining the Hebrew-to-English translation of this verse.

How is pride often manifested?

_____

_____

APPLY Will you briefly describe a time when you have rebelled and intentionally sinned?

_____

_____

Do you think pride played a part your in actions? If yes, why?

_____

_____

_____

For myself, I wanted to show God I was the boss. I didn't like how He was handling things, so I intentionally took matters into my own hands. I can remember thinking, _I'll show You God. . . . Just watch this. . . . Ha!_ Pride with a haughty spirit pervaded my thinking—which inevitably led to a precipitous fall!

Let's study a definition of problematic pride.

> **Pride:** _Undue confidence in and attention to one's own skills, accomplishments, state, possessions, or position. Pride is easier to recognize than to define, easier to recognize in others than in oneself. Many biblical words describe this concept, each with its own emphasis. Some of the synonyms for pride include arrogance, presumption, conceit, self-satisfaction, boasting, and high-mindedness. It is the opposite of humility, the proper attitude one should have in relation to God._[8]

Just for thought, why do you think pride is easier to recognize in others than in oneself?

_____

_____

"When pride comes, then comes disgrace, but with humility comes wisdom."

Proverbs 11:2

Word Study
PRIDE

The word "pride" in Proverbs 11:2 is translated from the Hebrew word _zadon,_ which means "to be arrogant, contemptuous" or filled with "pride, haughtiness, arrogance," or "conceit." Often manifested by rebellion and intentional sin.[7]

Although we have researched the negative aspects of the word "pride" there is also a positive aspect to pride. Read the following verses and note how they use the "pride" in a beneficial sense.

> *"And he took great pride in the ways of the Lord and again removed the high places and the Asherim from Judah."* (2 Chronicles 17:6 NASB)

> *"We are not trying to commend ourselves to you again, but are giving you an opportunity to take pride in us, so that you can answer those who take pride in what is seen rather than in what is in the heart."* (2 Corinthians 5:12)

APPLY What in your life makes you proud in the best sense of the word?

_____

_____

_____

I am extremely proud of my husband and my children. They create in me a positive form of pride. Although I cannot be proud because of my own accomplishments in their lives, I can be filled with pride in what the Lord has done within them. I am proud of how each of them live lives of integrity.

📖 Read the following proverbs and note what harm can come from the negative type of pride.

Proverbs 13:10

_____

Proverbs 16:5

_____

Proverbs 16:18

_____

Proverbs 18:12

_____

Oswald Chambers comments on pride in *My Utmost for His Highest*. He says, "There are areas of self-will in our lives where our pride pours contempt on the throne of God. . . . If we trust in our abilities instead of God's we produce consequences for which God will hold us responsible."[9]

  APPLY Have you or do you know of someone who you believe God held responsible for their prideful actions?

_____

_____

So, what is the opposite of pride? It's humility. God wants us to learn how to be a humble people. Let's look at the contrast of pride with humility. From the next proverbs match the benefits that occur from a person learning humility.

Proverbs 3:34	wealth, honor, life
Proverbs 15:33	honor
Proverbs 22:4	grace

HELP FOR THE OVER-BURDENED

"Come to Me, all you who labor and are heavy-laden and overburdened, and I will cause you to rest. [I will ease and relieve and refresh your souls.] Take My yoke upon you and learn of Me, for I am gentle (meek) and humble (lowly) in heart, and you will find rest (relief and ease and refreshment and recreation and blessed quiet) for your souls. For My yoke is wholesome (useful, good—not harsh, hard, sharp, or pressing, but comfortable, gracious, and pleasant), and My burden is light and easy to be borne." (Matthew 11:28–30 The Amplified Bible)

Did You Know?
YOKE

A yoke is a heavy wooden harness that fits over the shoulders of two beasts. Usually, one well-experienced animal is yoked to a slightly smaller and inexperienced animal. The stronger and more knowledgeable animal guides, leads, and trains the other partner it is yoked with. It tends to carry more of the weight of the yoke, so that most of the burden is lifted off the inexperienced one.

Contentment

DAY THREE

As you read the above proverbs, think of how the benefits of humility have the capabilities to produce contentment.

📖 Please read Matthew 11:28–30 in the margin. Please circle the words in these verses that you would consider reflective of personal contentment?

Don't the words "ease," "refreshment," "recreations," "comfortable," "gracious," "pleasant," and "blessed quiet" bring to mind a picture of contentment? (Did I hear a mom of preschoolers shout a hearty, "Amen" to the "blessed quiet"?

 As we close today, will you choose to take the yoke of humility and contentment on your shoulders? Ask God to remove your pride and replace it with His yoke.

Today's Heart-Print
"Humility and the fear of the LORD bring wealth and honor and life."
(Proverbs 22:4)

Dear Father,

_____

_____

_____

_____

_____

_____

_____

_____

_____

RAVENOUS ENVY

As iron is eaten away by rust, so the envious are consumed by their own passion.
—Antisthenes[10]

A few years ago, a beautiful woman at my children's school worked as a teacher's assistant. She envied almost anyone that crossed her path. She envied the teacher's position. Her jealousy surfaced when others received praise for a job well done. She hated any women whom she perceived to be prettier than herself. She attempted to displace the principal's wife by at first by flirting covertly. When flirting failed to achieve her purpose, she propositioned him with a romantic getaway weekend. He said, no and reported her behavior to the school district. Within a few weeks, she was transferred to another school with a warning to cease any further contact with the former principal.

This talented and attractive woman could not move past what she perceived others had that she did not. Her envy ended up destroying almost every relationship in her life. Her discontent with her self ended up costing her job, her marriage, and many, many friendships.

Envy can rear its ugly head in so many ways. Today, we will investigate envy and jealousy through the eyes of Scripture. We're going to read the story of two women who allowed jealousy to consume the contentment they possessed.

First, let's read Proverbs 14:30 in the margin.

 This proverb states that peace and contentment give life to the body, but envy rots the bones. How would you explain what this means to someone else? Have you ever felt so envious that it felt like it came from the core of your soul?

_____

_____

_____

List ten things that women might envy other women over.

1. _____   6. _____
2. _____   7. _____
3. _____   8. _____
4. _____   9. _____
5. _____   10. _____

My list of envy includes: thinness, attractiveness, money, career, ministry, children, educations, travel, home, and clothing. Those are just a few of my top items. Do you relate to any on my list?

Envy can hit with no warning. Like a tsunami, waves of rivalry can engulf us in destructive attitudes and behaviors. Today we are going to study Leah and Rachel. I want you to try to experience the female competitiveness throughout the story. Read slowly and notice the descriptive words used to display the jealousy the two sisters held toward each other.

To begin read Genesis 29:14-19. What is the first thing we discover as a difference between Leah and Rachel?

_____

_____

Leah had weak eyes, but Rachel was lovely in form and beautiful. No one knows for sure what the term "weak eyes" means; some commentaries suggest a condition of crossed eyes or nearsightedness. However, read the following thoughts from the *Bible Background Commentary.*

> In the comparative description of Rachel and Leah, the only comment about Leah concerns her eyes. The term used is generally considered positive and speaks of fragility, vulnerability, tenderness or a delicate quality (NIV note). Although eyes were a principal component of beauty in the ancient world, Leah's positive features paled in comparison to Rachel's loveliness.[11]

It is possible that Leah was an attractive woman; however, her sister outshone her in the good looks department.

"A heart at peace gives life to the body, but envy rots the bones."

Proverbs 14:30

My Heart's Cry:

Father, please nudge me at the first sign of envy creeping into my life over someone else's blessings. I want to learn to rejoice with others over their blessings. In Jesus' name, Amen.

Do you think that Leah grew up comparing herself to the beauty of Rachel? Why or why not?

_____

_____

_____

Word Study
ENVY

Envy: ardent zeal, jealousy, anger, indignations. The jealousy of love is declared to as "unyielding as the grave" in Song of Songs 8:6.[12]

📖 Well let's examine how much further these two sisters travel down "rivalry road." Continue to read Genesis 29:28–30.

What a mess! Jacob ends up married to both women. According to these verses, what would increase the rivalry between Leah and Rachel?

_____

_____

But there's more to this story. Read Genesis 29:31–35. Who seems to have the advantage at this point of the story? Why?

_____

_____

📖 Read Proverbs 30:21–23. How does verse 23 apply to Leah?

_____

_____

How does Genesis 30:1 describe Rachel's reaction to the birth of her nephew?

_____

_____

Rachel's fury broke upon Jacob. (Teach him to have two wives!) Let's go back and read a proverb that could apply to this situation. Take a moment to read Proverbs 6:32–35. Although this proverb speaks of adultery and a husband's fury, how would this apply to Leah, Rachel, and Jacob?

_____

_____

Allow me to paraphrase this proverb for you in a way that incorporates Rachel and Leah's story:

"For jealousy arouses Rachel's fury, and she will show no mercy when she takes revenge. She will not accept any compensation."

I don't think anything that Jacob could have done for Rachel would have diminished the envy she felt toward Leah. It seems that the tables have turned in Leah's favor, driving Rachel to maddening jealousy. Yet, as we read in Genesis 30:1–24, the saga continues. As you read this Scripture passage, make notations in your Bibles beside any phrases that convey the bitterness held between the two women. I will give you the first two.

Verse 6: "God has vindicated me."
Verse 8: "I have had a great struggle with my sister."

Verse: 9

Verse 10:

Verse 15:

Verse 19:

Verse 23:

Quite a dysfunctional family wouldn't you say? How does this story apply to Proverbs 27:4?

_____

_____

Can you describe a time when you felt overwhelming jealousy? Although, I am not envious by nature (I have plenty of other faults), I know occasionally the green-eyed monster of envy rears its ugly head in my Christian walk. Oddly, the root of my jealousy springs from my desire to please God. I want Him to smile down and see just how wonderfully I work in His kingdom. I long to be a super-saint for God.

Unfortunately, it seems this malady runs deep within the Christian community. Do you remember the story in Mark 9 when Jesus' disciples were strolling into Capernaum and they argued about who was the greatest? Mark writes, "When he [Jesus] was in the house, he asked them, 'What were you arguing about on the road?' But they kept quiet because on the way they had argued about who was the greatest."

In our human nature, we all want to surpass those around us; even the disciples who walked with Jesus were not content in their blessed position. They wanted to be the greatest. Our jealousies run the gamut of our desires, ranging from beauty, to children, to money, to even our Christian faith.

Now take some time to read James 3:14–16. According to these verses, where does envy originate?

_____

_____

Yes, right from the devil. Do you remember from yesterday's lesson the fact that Satan desired to be like The Most High?

Take a few moments to consider the things that provoke envy and jealousy in you. Write a prayer asking God to dig out the root of envy.

Today's Heart-Print
"A heart at peace gives life to the body, but envy rots the bones."
(Proverbs 14:30)

Oh Most High God,

_____

_____

_____

_____

_____

> **"Anger is cruel and fury overwhelming, but who can stand before jealousy."**
>
> **Proverbs 27:4**

GUILT-FREE CONTENTMENT

How tedious is a guilty conscience—John Webster[13]

The U.S. Treasury manages a number of special collections, including the Conscience Fund. This fund accepts donations from those who have cheated on their taxes or stolen from the government. In one letter that came with a $10 donation, a woman wrote that her younger brother had stolen a pair of scissors from his government job. He gave the scissors to his sister before he died; she felt guilt over the "inheritance."[14]

Another story the I.R.S. relays is of receiving an anonymous contribution for over $500.00. They received it with a note explaining, "I have not been able to sleep at night ever since I cheated on a past tax return. So, here is some of the money. If I still can't sleep, I'll send you the rest."[15]

Lack of contentment often follows an act of dishonesty. The Book of Proverbs has much to say about integrity and honesty. I think we can learn much from some proverbs in today's lesson to help us find a new depth of contentment.

📖 Read Proverbs 10:9 and 11:3. How would these verses exemplify a person's ability to find contentment? Will you paraphrase these verses using the word "contentment"?

_____

_____

_____

Now read a different version of Proverb 10:9 in the side margin.

As you read this passage in the sidebar, underline the two words that seem to lay the foundation for contentment. Circle the word that embodies the destruction of contentment.

America's beloved President, Abraham Lincoln, possessed a quiet confidence. His friends and acquaintances said he exuded an inner contentment even during the most difficult crisis. His nickname, Honest Abe, might be a clue to his satisfaction in life. The following two anecdotes tell us how he would not allow himself to wait until the very next morning to correct even the most unintentional of dishonest acts.

One story states that predates Lincoln's presidency has Honest Abe discovering late one afternoon after counting the cash in his store, that he had taken a few more cents from a customer than he should have. He immediately closed the store, and walked a long distance to give back the overcharge.

On another occasion, he determined he had miscalculated the weight of tea a woman had purchased the night before. As soon as he realized his mistake, he weighed out the remaining amount of tea that should have been given to the customer and carried it to the unsuspecting woman's home.[16]

📖 Read Leviticus 19:35. Did Lincoln obey the instruction in this verse? If yes, how?

My Heart's Cry:

Lord God, I long for contentment. Reveal to me any of my own thoughts or actions that keep my contentment at bay. Let my contentment rest on the foundation of godly integrity and honesty. Amen.

"Honesty lives confident and carefree, but Shifty is sure to be exposed."

**Proverbs 10:9
(The Message)**

_____

_____

_____

📖 Read the following proverbs and note why Lincoln might have possessed a foundation of confidence and peace.

Proverbs 11:1

_____

Proverbs 16:11

_____

Proverbs 20:23.

_____

I believe President Lincoln had contentment because he lived his life right-
eously and honestly. Living with integrity positions a safeguard in our lives.
When we use opportunities to reveal our honesty, it creates more situations
to honor God. The flip side is that when we squander such opportunities,
we bring reproach or dishonor to God. Each decision you make to obey
God's Word and His Spirit's leading will bring a greater sense of peace in
your life, while each decision to disobey will bring confusion and destruction. Obedience brings the greatest safety and security.

📖 Read the proverbs listed below. Then write the phrase that promotes
contentment and make note of what displeases the Lord.

Proverbs 10:16

_____

Proverbs 11:8

_____

Proverbs 12:3

_____

Proverbs 12:12

_____

Proverbs 17:15

_____

Proverbs 21:8

_____

Proverbs 24:24

_____

Did You Know?
CROOKED DEALING

In the beginning, people bartered instead
of using money. Bartering is the exchange
of a good or service for another good or
service. For example, a bag of rice traded
for a bag of beans. Usually scales and
weights were used to render the amount
of the trade. However, dishonest mer-
chants used two different sets of weight
to increase their profits. Lighter stones
were placed on the scales when selling
so that a lesser quantity was sold for the
stated price. And then on the other end
of the deal, heavier ones were placed on
the scales when buying so they could
purchase more for the same price.

Place a check by the following situations that might have occurred. Write down what the righteous response should have been.

❏ You realize the clerk in the store gave you too much money back.

❏ Your waiter forgets to charge you for dessert.

❏ You bump your car into a parked vehicle.

❏ You realize a co-worker was blamed for your mistake.

One day I backed into someone's car in a parking lot. Sitting in my van, I told myself, "no one will ever know." My husband is an insurance agent, and I knew he would not be happy with me. However, I was also a Women's ministry director for our church. The battle raged within, but integrity won out. Entering different offices, I inquired if anyone owned a white Toyota Camry. Finally, I found the owner, and he threw a screaming fit when he learned that I had hit his car. But oh well, I slept better that night knowing I had done the right thing by searching him out.

Word Study
RIGHTEOUS

The Hebrew word for *righteous* (*saddiyq*) can also mean "just," "lawful," "honest," "right." *Saddiyq* is often used in Scripture to describe the Lord's character. God is "righteous in all His ways" (Psalm 145:17). God Himself is therefore the standard of all ethics and morality. *Saddiyq* also portrays a person who is honest with others.[17]

"The Lord despises the deeds of the wicked but loves those who try to be good."

Proverbs 15:9 (TLB)

📖 Read the following proverbs and list the given benefits for those who act in integrity and righteousness.

Proverbs 4:18

_____

Proverbs 10:24

_____

Proverbs 11:23

_____

Proverbs 15:9

_____

Proverbs 15:29

_____

📖 Compare Proverbs 11:18 with 1 Timothy 6:6. What truth do we find in each of these verses?

_____
_____
_____
_____
_____

 Memorize 1 Timothy 6:6, which is our Heart-Print for today. And then, let's ask God to help us understand how the principle of righteousness and integrity equals contentment.

Today's Heart-Print
"But godliness with contentment is great gain." (1 Timothy 6:6)

Father God,

_____

_____

_____

_____

_____

_____

_____

_____

Extra Mile
FATHER ABRAHAM

Discover the benefit of believing God. Read Genesis 12:1–9 and Genesis 15:1–6. Now examine Romans 4:3 and James 2:23. What did Abraham do that God credited it to him as righteousness?

IT IS WELL WITH MY SOUL

Contentment

DAY FIVE

Where there is peace, God is.—George Herbert[18]

A tragic fire burned Chicago to a city of cinders in 1871. Thousands were left homeless, hundreds died in the fire and its aftermath. Horatio Gates Spafford, a lawyer, had invested most of his earnings in the city. Though he suffered financially as a result of the fire, he still aided the people of Chicago in many ways. He assisted with clothing, food, and preached the good news of Jesus to many desperate people.

Finally after two years, Mr. Spafford and his family decided to take a vacation to Europe where he would join the evangelist Dwight Moody. Suddenly, delayed by business Spafford determined to send his wife and four daughters on ahead to Europe. He told them he would catch up with them shortly. The women boarded the ship, Ville du Havre, and they waved good-bye to their husband and daddy.

The loved ones of Mr. Spafford never made it to Europe. The ship collided with another sailing ship near Newfoundland. The ship sank quickly. In less than twenty minutes, Anna the mother, found herself clinging to a floating piece of wreckage. From hundreds of passengers only forty-seven survived. The Spafford's young daughters had drowned as the ship sunk.

Mr. Spafford received the horrific telegram from his wife. On it were typed two words. "Saved. Alone." He boarded the next available ship to be near his distraught wife. As the ship sailed near the area of the tragedy, he penned the words to the beloved hymn, "It Is Well With My Soul."[19]

> *When peace, like a river, attendeth my way,*
> *When sorrows like sea billows roll;*
> *Whatever my lot, Thou has taught me to say,*
> *It is well, it is well, with my soul.*

Mr. Stafford had peace regardless of his circumstances. Do you?

📖 Let's look at the issue of peace. Read Proverbs 14:30a.

My Heart's Cry:

Lord, I praise You for the peace that You give me. Thank You that no matter what happens today or tomorrow that You are my Prince of Peace. Help me to remember that as long as I trust You all will be well with my soul. In Jesus' name, Amen.

Extra Mile

LIFE IS FULL OF TROUBLE

The Bible doesn't promise us our lives will be trouble free. Read John 16:33 and then read Job 1 and 2. What amazing thing do we discover in Job 1:22? What did Job say to his wife in 2:10? Write down Job 1:22 followed by Job 23:10. Ponder how you would respond to Horatio Spafford's or Job's tragedies.

What does this peace do for us?

_____

_____

📖 Read Proverbs 12:25a; Proverbs 17:22.

If a heart at peace gives life what happens to a person with an anxious heart and a crushed spirit?

Is there something producing a crushed spirit in you today?

_____

Let's take a look at few various verses throughout the Bible to discover more about peace. Jot down what you discover about finding peace in our lives.

Isaiah 9:6

_____

_____

John 14:27

_____

_____

Romans 5:1

_____

_____

Philippians 4:7

_____

_____

2 Thessalonians 3:16

_____

_____

From our reading of Scripture, we learn that true peace is found when we are in relationship with Jesus Christ. However, we also must do our part. Do you recall in yesterday's study that if we act in righteousness, we should find contentment.

📖 Read Isaiah 32:17 and discover what the fruit of righteousness is.

Our relationship with Jesus produces integrity within us, which results in peace, quietness, and confidence forever. I believe Horatio Spafford discovered the truth of this when he heard of the tragic accident at sea. Life's sorrow did not steal his peace. His peace could not be taken from him. Is it well with your soul today?

"Peace I leave with you; my peace I give you. I do not give to you as the world gives. Do not let your hearts be troubled and do not be afraid."

John 14:27

Today's Heart-Print
"The fruit of righteousness will be peace; the effect of righteousness will be quietness and confidence forever." (Isaiah 32:17)

Your Heart's Impression

Journal your thoughts about:

The wisdom of finding contentment in your life.

_____

_____

_____

What in life causes you the most discontentment?

_____

_____

_____

Journal your thoughts about Paul's words, *"godliness with contentment is great gain"* (1 Timothy 6:6).

_____

_____

_____

_____

List five blessings in your life and why you are grateful for them.

_____

_____

_____

_____

_____

Tell the Lord God what is in your heart after this week's lesson.
Lord God,

_____

_____

_____

_____

_____

_____

_____

_____

_____

1. Frank S. Mead, *12,000 Religious Quotations*, (Grand Rapids, MI: Baker Book House, 1989), 87.

2. Edward K Rowell & *Leadership Journal, 1001 Quotes, Illustrations, and Humorous Stories for Preachers, Teachers, & Writers* (Grand Rapids, MI: Baker Books, 1996), 39.

3. *NIV Hebrew-Greek Study Bible* (Chattanooga, TN: AMG Publishers, 1996). Old Testament Lexical Aids, #2273, 1516.

4. Max Anders, *Holman Old Testmament Comentary-Proverbs* (Nashville, TN Holman Reference, 2005). 137.

5. Ibid, 994.

6. Walter. C Kaiser, Peter H. Davids, F. F. Bruce, Manfred. T Brauch, *Hard Sayings of the Bible* (Downer's Grove, IL: InterVarsity Press, 1996), 316.

7. *NIV Hebrew-Greek Study Bible* (Chattanooga, TN: AMG Publishers, 1996), Old Testament Lexical Aids, #2295, 1512.

8. *Holman Bible Dictionary*, Copyright © 1991 Holman Bible Publishers. In NavPress Bible Software database.

9. Oswald Chambers, *My Utmost for His Highest: An Updated Version in Today's Language* (Grand Rapids, MI: Discovery House Publishers, 1991), 12/28.

10. http://www.whatquote.com/quotes/Antisthenes/7842-As-iron-is-eaten-awa.htm

11. John H. Walton and Victor H. Matthews, *The IVP Bible Background Commentary*: *Genesis-Deuteronomy*. In NavPress Bible Software Database © 1998.

12. *NIV Hebrew-Greek Study Bible,* Old Testament Lexical Aids, #7863, 1548.

13. http://www.bartleby.com/47/4/55.html

14. Brendan Miniter, "To Uncle Sam With Love," *Wall Street Journal, Editorial Page,* 15 April 2002.

15. Max Anders, *Holman Old Testmament Comentary-Proverbs,* 182.

16. James B. McClure. *Anecotes and Stories of Abraham Lincoln: Early Life Stories, Professional Life Stories, White House Stories, War Stories, Miscellaneous Stories.* (Mechanicsburg, PA: Stockpole Classic Reprint, 2006), 22–36. Originally Published 1888.

17. *NIV Hebrew-Greek Study Bible*, Old Testament Lexical Aids, #7404, 1545.

18. Frank S. Mead, *2,000 Religious Quotations*, *Inspiring Hymn Stories for Daily Devotions* (Grand Rapids, MI: Kregel Publications, 190), 202.

19. Kenneth Blanchard, *Servant Leader* (Nashville, TN: J. Countryman, a Division of Thomas Nelson, Inc., 2003), 26.

Heart-Print of Friendship

*Friendship is unnecessary, like philosophy, like art.... It has no survival value;
rather it is one of those things that give value to survival.*—C. S. Lewis[1]

Friends. They come in all shapes and sizes. Some have big hearts. A few deliver the sunshine of laughter. One may offer a slender shoulder for you to cry on. One ally might listen while you whine, another may speak the truth even when it hurts. One buddy may bring a casserole when you're sick, still another offers a prayer for healing. Pals will compliment you, hug you, watch your kids, and send you a birthday card. Or they might call once a year just to catch up on life. Whichever type of friends filter through your life, true, healthy friendships are a gift from God.

We learn the importance of friendship at a very early age. I remember my friend's three-year-old daughter throwing out the worst insult she could conceive. Her little freckled face in a scowl, she would growl "You no my friend!"

Throughout our lives, we long for true friendship. This fact is supported by the television shows that we loyally have tuned into throughout the decades. We hum lyrics from the *Cheers* theme song "Sometimes you want to go, Where everybody knows your name, and they're always glad you came." We watch *Friends* with hopes we can find enduring relationships too. We purchase DVDs of *Seinfeld* because the characters have become our friends over the years.

During this week's lesson, the heart-print of friendship will help us not only to develop good friends, but also to become better friends to others. We will discover that not all our chums are true friends. But most importantly, we'll learn how to develop an intimate relationship with God who will be our best friend forever.

Whichever type of friends filter through your life, true, healthy friendships are a gift from God.

KNIT TOGETHER

Blessed are they who have the gift of making friends, for it is one of God's best gifts. It involves many things, but above all, the power of going out of one's self and appreciating whatever is noble and loving in another.—Thomas Hughes[2]

I knocked hesitantly on the white painted door. I thought to myself, *What in the world am I doing here! I feel so stupid. I have never even laid eyes on this woman.* As I waited for the door to open, I recalled how this predicament came about.

The women's ministries director at my church had called asking me if I would mentor a new Christian woman. She explained to me that the woman, Connie, accepted Christ about a year ago. Connie now felt she needed someone to step her through the basics of her new found faith. Another woman had attempted to mentor her, but with busy schedules, it had not worked out for either of them. I agreed to meet with her and instruct her through a small study on the beginning principles of Christianity.

However, God not only desired Connie to be tutored—he had an additional plan—friendship. He forged a friendship between the two of us. You see, He not only saw Connie's need, He had heard my private prayers for a close girlfriend and a friend who loved Jesus. I desperately longed for someone who I could laugh and weep with through the drama of life. (Not to mention, someone who could put up with me!)

So when the stranger, Connie, opened the door to my timid knock, little did either one of us realize that a friendship of the souls would transpire. But God knew, because He is the author of friendship. He wants us to develop healthy relationships to help us through this time we share on earth.

Before we jump into our study on friendship, first will you write down your own definition of what friendship means to you?

_____

_____

_____

📖 Read Proverbs 17:17. According to this proverb what is the primary function of a friend?

_____

_____

In the margin, read how *The Amplified Bible* words Proverbs 17:17.

When I read the Amplified Version, I can see where a friend can be just like family. As for myself, I love a few of my friends more than a couple of my family members. You know how family can be, well, . . . "family."

Friendship comes in all shapes and sizes. Many times, we don't realize we might have a true friend in someone until time goes by. These complex relations ebb and flow like the tide. I always chuckle when I read J. R. R. Tolkien's words in

My Heart's Cry:

Father God, help me to remember in the busyness of life the value of friendships. Remind me that You gave the gift of friendship for us to bless and encourage one another in the joys and sorrows of life. Amen.

"A friend loves at all times, and is born as is a brother, for adversity."

Proverbs 17:17 (The Amplified Bible)

The Fellowship of the Ring, when Bilbo Baggins says, "I don't know half of you half as well as I should like; and I like less than half of you half as well as you deserve." Yes, all these multifaceted companionships need to be studied so that we can understand why and how God designed friendly relationships in our lives.

📖 Read the following proverbs and then note the attribute it denotes for friendship.

Proverbs 17:9a

_____

Proverbs 18:24b

_____

Proverbs 27:6a

_____

Proverbs 27:9b

_____

A true friend offers earnest counsel, but tells the truth even when it hurts. A good friend forgives and remains loyal. I would like for us now to examine a biblical example of friendship.

📖 Read 1 Samuel 18:1 in the margin.

I love the phrase "knit with the soul of David." Years ago, I used to knit and crochet. It amazed me then and still does how one long, stringy piece of yarn can produce scarves, baby blankets, mittens, or slippers, all by just looping the yarn correctly. *Webster's Dictionary* gives various definitions of the term *knit*: "to interlock loops of yarn; to join closely and firmly; to grow together as in broken bones."[3] In what ways would you describe how friendships are knit together?

_____

_____

_____

Let's study a bit more about the biblical example of the friendship of Jonathan and David.

📖 Read 1 Samuel 20. Now let's examine the interaction between these two men.

Describe the conflict in verses 1–3.

_____

_____

How did Jonathan respond to David in verse 4?

_____

_____

> "... the soul of Jonathan was knit with the soul of David, and Jonathan loved him as his own soul."
>
> (1 Samuel 18:1 KJV)

In David's emotional upheaval, what did he suggest to Jonathan in verses 8–10?

_____

_____

_____

How did Jonathan respond to David's outburst in verses 12–16?

_____

_____

_____

What special request did Jonathan make to David in 14–15?

_____

_____

_____

Describe the conclusion to this chapter given in verse 42.

_____

_____

_____

During their friendship, Jonathan and David embodied the teachings regarding friendship in the Book of Proverbs. Although emotions and feelings ran high, both men recognized the loyalty and honesty of the other. So much so that Jonathan said, he was willing to give up his rightful inheritance of the kingdom for the love of his friend, David.

📖 In the end, Jonathan was killed in battle, and David became King of Israel. Let's look briefly at David's response to the death of Jonathan. Read 2 Samuel 1:11–12. Describe David's reaction to the news.

_____

_____

_____

📖 Now read 2 Samuel 9:1–10. How did David uphold his covenant of friendship with Jonathan?

_____

_____

📖 Read Proverbs 19:22a and then fill in the blank space on the question below.

What a man desires is _____.

Do you think the friendship of Jonathan and David fulfilled Proverbs 19:22a? Explain why or why not?

_____

_____

Read what Matthew Henry writes concerning this friendship:

The friendship of David and Jonathan was the effect of Divine grace, which produces in true believers one heart and one soul, and causes them to love each other. This union of souls is from partaking in the Spirit of Christ. Where God unites hearts, carnal matters are too weak to separate them.[4]

📖 Please reread Proverbs 17:17 and then briefly describe how this proverb fits the definition of friendship offered by Matthew Henry.

_____

_____

_____

Well, we have already covered quite a few verses in this lesson. I pray that you have discovered some new truth about friendship. At the beginning of Day One, I told you about my initial get-together with my friend, Connie. Although, I didn't know it, she was to become my "Jonathan." We have traveled many roads in our friendship. Our friendship is steadfast and enduring—a gift from God.

 Perhaps today you are longing for a friendship where you feel knit together. Or perhaps, you have been blessed with such a friend, but she has moved away. Ask God to bring you that type of friend. And then wait and watch. You never know, you might be called to knock on a stranger's door. It wasn't until I prayed for a companion of that caliber did God bring her into my life.

Today's Heart-Print
"What a man desires is unfailing love." (Proverbs 19:22a)

Father,

_____

_____

_____

_____

_____

RECIPE FOR FRIENDSHIP

Friendship

A friend will strengthen you with his prayers, bless you with his love and encourage you with his hope.—Unknown[5]

Monika lived alone; she felt alone. After a recent move to Nevada where she knew no one, disasters seemed to strike faster than she could have ever imagined. Her husband developed terminal cancer and died within months of the new move. She lost her beloved dog. Then she was diagnosed with an aggressive cancer. Her children lived across the country. She didn't know her neighbors very well. Monika felt alone, because she was alone.

My Heart's Cry:

Father, open my eyes to others who might need my friendship in bona fide actions. Show me how to be a first-class friend to anyone that is hurting and lonely. Lord, give me the understanding of the recipe for true friendships. Amen.

However, God in His faithfulness developed faithful friends and neighbors to help see her through the darkness that fell on her life. She says,

> At my lowest point, I knew how the apostle Paul felt when he said, "We were under great pressure, far beyond our ability to endure, so that we despaired even of life" (2 Corinthians 1:8). I echoed his refrain. Yet, new friends came to aid me. Old friends phoned and sent cards to encourage me. What would I have done without my friends?"

Monika's friends saved her from complete desolation. But what made those people react as friends? What personality characteristics enabled them to transition from uninterested acquaintances to helpful companions? These are the questions we will answer today.

What does Proverbs 27:10 advise us not to do?

_____

_____

_____

It advises us not to abandon or forget friends or our family's friends. This thought brings to mind the old song we hear every New Year's Eve, "Auld Lang Syne." Do you have any idea what those three words mean? Auld Lang Syne translates into modern English as "Old Long Ago." Many of our friendships seem a long time ago. I guess we could join in the chorus and sing,

Should old acquaintance be forgot and never brought to mind?
Should old acquaintance be forgot and days of auld lang syne?

And we would be paraphrasing Proverbs 27:10.

Review the word *friend* in the side margin. Below is a list of the stages of life. Under the appropriate stages, list the names of old friends that fit the sidebar definitions and descriptions.

Preschool

_____

Elementary School

_____

Middle School

_____

High School

_____

College and/or career

_____

Neighbors

_____

Did you have fond flashbacks? I did. My list included my preschool cousin, Annette. I smiled when I recalled my elementary school best friend, Karen. We played "kick the can," played with Barbies®, and tattled on one another. I also listed those brief tumultuous friends of middle school. These friendships ran hot or cold. One day we all dressed alike—twinnies we said. The next day, they ditched me after school for the new girl in the class. Throughout my life, friends have played an important role in developing my character (Both good and bad). It's amazing how many friends cross our path during a lifetime isn't it? As I completed my list, I could recall names of many friends, but others I could just see a shadow of a face.

 So maybe we should try to contact a few of these old buddies. Recently I saw a great quote on the inside of a Dove® chocolate wrapper. It read, "If old acquaintance be forgot, give them a call and remember." Why don't we each make a list of old pals we would like to reunite with in the near future?

1. _____

2. _____

3. _____

The names of those I remembered all held certain character traits that stood out in our relationship together. I would guess that applies to your list of old buddies as well. Let's peek at a few proverbs to gain wisdom on what makes a good companion.

📖 Read Proverbs 27:9

A great friendship can bring joy to the heart just like perfume and incense. It also speaks of a pleasant friend. Please match the proverb with a correct attribute.

Proverbs 10:12	faithful
Proverbs 15:17	honest answer
Proverbs 16:13	speaks the truth
Proverbs 12:25	covers wrongs
Proverbs 20:6	a kind word
Proverbs 24:26	love

As you can see, the Bible puts a lot of emphasis on honesty, love, and faithfulness. I do, too. However, let's brainstorm for a few other traits we value in friendships. Can you think of any others that would be high on your priority list for friendship?

_____

_____

On the next page are a few that came to my mind. Please review the following list of possible friendship traits; number them according to what you value the most, # 1 being the most important. And then, jot down the names of the friends you listed by their friendship traits.

___ kind	___ fun-loving
___ humorous	___ honest
___ compassionate	___ loyal
___ full of integrity	___ thoughtful
___ loving	___ helpful

TWO ARE BETTER THAN ONE

"Two are better than one, because they have a good return for their work: If one falls down, his friend can help him up. But pity the man who falls and has no one to help him up! Also, if two lie down together, they will keep warm. But how can one keep warm alone? Though one may be overpowered, two can defend themselves. A cord of three strands is not quickly broken." (Ecclesiastes 4:9–12)

📖 Please read Ecclesiastes 4:9–12 in the side margin. Will you paraphrase these verses in your own words?

_____

_____

_____

_____

_____

Now let's take a quick look at one final verse. Please read Genesis 2:18 and fill in the blanks.

"The Lord God said, "It is _____ for the man to be alone. I will make a _____ suitable for him."

Although this verse describes God creating a wife for Adam, I believe the general premise is that human beings are not to be solitary creatures. We were created for fellowship with God and other people. Considering this, who might be the third chord in any type of friendship described in Ecclesiastes 4:12?

_____

_____

APPLY In my personal experience, the friends who share a love of God become my strongest friends. Have you found this to be true in your life?

_____

_____

_____

Friends and neighbors who hold these qualities can become our lifeline through the difficulties of life.

Today's Heart-Print
"If one falls down, his friend can help him up. But pity the man who falls and has no one to help him up!" (Ecclesiastes 4:10)

Lord God,

_____

_____

_____

_____

_____

_____

_____

_____

_____

INSIDE OUTSIDE

Friendship is always a sweet responsibility, never an opportunity.
—Kahil Gibran[6]

When I look in the mirror, I see all sorts of things. Freckles, wrinkles, large, blue eyes, whitened teeth, colored hair, etc. Sometimes I put on make-up just to cover the flaws. A good foundation does wonders for sun-damaged skin. With a little mascara and a touch of lipstick, I become presentable to the world.

But inside I might still harbor ugly attitudes of bitterness and hurt feelings. I may look good on the outside, but remain quite homely inside. My internal beauty will affect my friendships with others. Yesterday we studied different friendship traits. Today we are going to look at the same attributes of friendship, but apply them to ourselves. Hopefully, we will be able to touch-up ourselves with a little scriptural makeover.

 The following are the same attributes of friendship we studied yesterday. Now let's apply them to ourselves. Place an X by the characteristics you bring to a friendship.

☐ kind   ☐ fun-loving
☐ humorous   ☐ honest
☐ compassionate   ☐ loyal
☐ full of integrity   ☐ thoughtful
☐ loving   ☐ helpful

Are there a couple characteristics you could ask God to help you with in an effort to become a better friend? If yes, circle the ones you would like to improve upon. But I want to take an honest look at some of these traits that we may feel strong in, but in reality may reveal a weakness in ourselves.

📖 Please read the following proverbs. Then make a note of what type of weakness each proverb denotes.

Proverbs 3:28	sarcasm
Proverbs 11:12	anger
Proverbs 22:24	betrayal
Proverbs 25:8–9	insincere flattery
Proverbs 26:18–19	ridicule/derision
Proverbs 29:5	withholding of help

Did you find something of which you are guilty? I know that sometimes I flatter people, so that I will gain something I want or need. And sarcasm was always one of my favorite weapons, when I wanted to hurt someone, but then I could say, "Hey, I was joking." More times than I care to admit, I have pretended I didn't notice when a friend needed my help. I battled anger for years, usually spewing it upon those I loved the most. Can you relate? Thankfully, God can cure us of these ills.

📖 Read Colossians 3:7–10.

My Heart's Cry:

Father, teach me how to be a better friend. Today reveal to me my strength's and my weakness in my friendship with others. In Jesus' name, Amen.

According to these verses what can prove harmful to our friendships?

_____

_____

_____

What do these verses advise us to do?

_____

_____

What words suggest that it is a continual process in our lives?

_____

_____

We are instructed to take off our old practices and to put on a new self. According to 2 Corinthians 5:17 why are we able to do this?

_____

_____

Because we are new in Christ Jesus! Doesn't that make you want to shout for joy? I can become a better friend, because I am a new creation. Let's take this a step further and see exactly what type of friendship traits we can obtain through Jesus.

📖 Read Colossians 3:12–14 in the margin. From these verses, list all the attributes that identify you as a devoted friend to others?

_____

_____

_____

_____

PUT ON LOVE!

"Clothe yourselves therefore, as God's own chosen ones (His own picked representatives), [who are] purified and holy and well-beloved [by God Himself, by putting on behavior marked by] tenderhearted pity and mercy, kind feeling, a lowly opinion of yourselves, gentle ways, [and] patience [which is tireless and long-suffering, and has the power to endure whatever comes, with good temper]. Be gentle and forbearing with one another and, if one has a difference (a grievance or complaint) against another, readily pardoning each other; even as the Lord has [freely] forgiven you, so must you also [forgive]. And above all these [put on] love and enfold yourselves with the bond of perfectness [which binds everything together completely in ideal harmony] (Colossians 3:12–14; The Amplified Bible)."

As I read through these traits, it brings tears to my eyes. I know I am still lacking in many areas regarding friendship, as I am learning daily that only Christ within me can make me a better friend as opposed to anything I do in my own power. When I look in the mirror of Scripture, I yearn to see in myself, humility, compassion, gentleness, kindness, and patience. I want to forgive freely others and most importantly, I want to learn to love them with a pure heart. Yet, only a surrendered walk with my Savior and submission to His Spirit's leading will make me more conscious of being a Christian friend. After all, it is Christ that best exemplifies the "friend that sticks closer than a brother" (see Proverbs 18:24), as He became the model for John 15:13: _"Greater love has no one than this, that he lay down his life for his friends."_

📖 Reread Proverbs 17:9a. Can you list a few offenses that you caused that your friends overlooked?

_____

_____

Fortunately, our friends look past most of our faults. Walker Percy said, "We love those who know the worst of us and don't turn their faces away."[7] In closing today let's read one final proverb.

Read Proverbs 22:11 and then fill in the blanks to help cement the concept of what makes a great friend.

"He who loves a _____ and whose _____ is _____ will have the king for his friend.

Take some time and meditate on today's lesson. Then ask the Lord God to help you become a better friend to those around you.

Today's Heart-Print
"He who loves a pure heart and whose speech is gracious will have the king for his friend." (Proverbs 22:11)

Lord God,

_____

_____

_____

_____

_____

_____

_____

_____

_____

Friendship
DAY FOUR

> **"We love those who know the worst of us and don't turn their faces away."**
> **—Walker Percy**

SIPS OF FRIENDSHIP

The glory of friendship is not the outstretched hand, nor the kindly smile, nor the joy of companionship; it is the spiritual inspiration that comes to one when you discover that someone else believes in you and is willing to trust you with a friendship.—
Ralph Waldo Emerson[8]

Watching the orange-yellow sunrise, I sipped slowly on a steaming cup of French Roast coffee. I lounged back knowing a full day of activity also rose before me. I asked myself, "Where and how in the world do I even begin today's tasks?" I felt the familiar sensation of being overwhelmed flood my tired body and weary soul; the caffeine hadn't helped.

The phone's ring jarred me back to attention. Grabbing the phone I heard, "Hi, it's Lisa. Remember when we ran into each other again in Georgia?"

Her question reminded me of an occasion where I had been racing to another appointment at a convention, when suddenly we bumped into one another. We didn't know each other well, but we both recalled our immediate connection with each other at a different conference the year before. We traded phone numbers and promised to chat soon, so we could catch on the happenings with our families and life goals.

My Heart's Cry:
Father, remind me to slow down enough in my busy life to enjoy good conversation with my girlfriends. And help me to remember to take time to really listen. Amen.

Now as I listened to her excitement over the phone about what Christ was doing in her life, I smiled to myself. I continued to sip my coffee and celebrate with her as she told one story after another of God's hand in her day-to-day life.

Yes, she was busy, too. Her full life consisted of a husband out-of-work, two small children, and her own career. Plus, her mother was recently diagnosed with a devastating illness. Yet, she bubbled with enthusiasm for God's continual provision and unexpected blessings.

We talked for a long time. We discussed life, books, and coffee. She is a coffee aficionado, too. Finally as I hung up the phone, I drained the last drop of brew from my cup. The sun shone high and bright in the sky. "Wow! The morning is almost gone," I thought. But somehow I didn't feel panicky; instead I felt renewed. The day's tasks didn't seem as daunting.

I continued to grin as I realized the tremendous refreshment and joy that phone call delivered to my anxious soul. Little did my friend realize how she encouraged me by telling me about the details of "God moments" in her busy life. I started my own day, not with a dread of all that needed to be accomplished but with an anticipation of watching for the God-orchestrated moments. Suddenly, I giggled. I realized I had just experienced one. Lisa's phone call refreshed me! God's refreshment poured through me with a pot of coffee and a sip of sweet friendship.

Friendships refresh us. They remind me of strong mugs of coffee. Not only do they infuse us with energy, but also they come in all flavors, strength, and brewing time, yet they need tender care lest they are broken. Today, just for fun, we are going to use the analogy of cups of coffee to help us find out more about friendships.

📖 In the margin read both versions of Proverbs 18:1

What does this verse mean to you and the value of friendship?

_____

_____

_____

We all need companions to walk the road of life. I tend to be introverted, so I prefer a few close friends to chat with on a regular basis. However, my extroverted husband loves lots of people and commotion. Neither way is right or wrong. In fact, Scripture points us to having a balance of different types of friendships.

📖 Jesus is always the best example for us to study. Let's take a look at His friends and see what information we can garner for our own lives. Read the following verses and place the amount of friends and companions that were with Jesus during His time on earth. Also, note the activities that they are mentioned doing.

Matthew 4:25—5:1

_____

Luke 10:1, 17

_____

> ## "He who separates himself seeks his own desire, He quarrels against all sound wisdom."
>
> ### Proverbs 18:1
> ### (NASB)

> ## "Loners who care only for themselves spit on the common good.
>
> ### Proverbs 18:1
> ### (The Message)

Luke 6:13

_____

Matthew 17:1; Mark 5:37; Mark 14:33

_____

John 19:26

_____

APPLY Jesus had quite an array of people that He interacted with during His life. So, how do you think that applies to us?

_____

_____

_____

I believe we are to have a wide variety of friends. We should belong to a local church, so that we have access to a group of people to befriend us. Joining civic service groups, sports teams, or other likeminded enthusiasts provide an outlet for our individual interests and hobbies. A Sunday school class or small group serves a purpose in providing a more intimate atmosphere where we can share our hearts and grow together in all areas of our life. And then, just as Jesus had, we need an inner circle of friends—friends who will love us through the good and bad times.

Okay, now think back to what we just learned about the friends of Jesus. Because not all friendships are created equal. I have discovered that just like cups of coffee, friends come in a myriad of varieties. Friendship manifests itself in varying degrees of strength and longevity. I am going to list a few different coffee drinks and the types of friends that might share similar characteristics. I want you to jot down a couple of names of friends, past or present, who might fit each description. (Be careful to honor others; you might want to use fictitious names or initials.)

Proverbs 25:17—The Decaf Friend
The decaf friend is the chum whom you enjoy chatting with on occasion, but the relationship doesn't give a strong boost to your day. The depth of the relationship feels shallow. I believe the crowds that followed Jesus were a good example of this type of friendship. Although pleasant, the friendship will never move past the superficial needs to real heart-to-heart conversations. Most friends fall into this category. Decaf friends are fun and needed. They give our lives balance and social equilibrium.

1. _____

2. _____

3. _____

Proverbs 18:24—The Espresso Friends
Some friendships turn out to be short and sweet. We find these buddies usually through group associations. They can be people we meet in a small group, co-workers, or perhaps a group of parents for a child's soccer team. Similar interests and functions bind these camaraderies together. I would guess the seventy-two disciples (Luke 10:1) that Jesus sent out fell in to this category of comrades.

Did You Know?
COFFEE LEGENDS

A coffee bean is really not a bean but a berry? It is actually a fruit. A legend dating back to 850 BC is told that a goat herder in Ethiopia noticed his goats were friskier after eating the red berries of a local shrub. He began to munch on the berries and felt happier himself. After much experimentation, the cup of coffee was developed to help give us a stimulating boost.

However, around AD 1100, coffee was believed by some Christians to be the devil's drink. Pope Vincent III wished to banish the drink. Before doing so, he decided to give it a try first. He delighted in the tasty drink so much that he acknowledged it a "blessed" drink and said, "Coffee is so delicious it would be a pity to let the infidels have exclusive use of it." Shortly thereafter, monks began to brew the drink at monasteries so they could stay awake during the long duration of prayer sessions.

The Decaf Friend:

"And when you find a friend, don't out-wear your welcome; show up at all hours and he'll soon get fed up."

**Proverbs 25:17
(The Message)**

The Espresso Friend:

"Friends come and friends go, but a true friend sticks by you like family."

**Proverbs 18:24
(The Message)**

The Cappuccino Friend:

"Friends love through all kinds of weather."

**Proverbs 17:17a
The Message**

1. _____
2. _____
3. _____

Proverbs 17:17a—The Cappuccino Friends

Cappuccino friends are important confidants. Jesus' twelve "inner circle" disciples are a good example of this type of friendship. Usually, we will have several of these at one time. These strong friendships endure with time and distance. A friend that exemplifies this pattern may be a girlfriend you chat with only a couple of times a year, but the deep love and trust you have for each other maintains the friendship. These friends strengthen and sharpen us with their good advice.

1. _____
2. _____
3. _____

Proverbs 27:17—The Latte Friends

Ah, "latte friends" are my favorite. These sweet, long-lasting relationships deliciously flavor my life. Usually, you will only come across three or four of these treasures during a lifetime. James, John, and Peter were "latte friends" for Jesus. These allies know and guard your secrets. They help you to see yourself for who you really are inside. They discern the good and the bad traits of your personality. "Latte friends" will tell you the truth; they speak the truth with kindness and love.

These invaluable companions in life will become your inner circle; in a sense they become spiritual soul mates. Sometimes these life companions become more like family than your own biological relatives. (Remember Jonathan and David?) "Latte friends" love you through all of life's joys and sorrows.

Sweet, long-lasting friendships brew over time. Their strength increases with relational experiences. The depth of relationship matures through life's uncertain circumstances. Savor your latte friends; they are a gift from heaven.

1. _____
2. _____
3. _____

I hope you had fun with this coffee illustration. I did. But now, unfortunately we need to study one last type of friendship. Unhealthy friendships. A few people, disguise themselves as essential friends, but can bring emotional and spiritual harm to us. As I said, I would be remiss, if I did not recognize the fact that not all our pals are beneficial friends.

In my life, I have encountered a few friendships that turned sour. They each left a pungent taste when the relationship evaporated. I call these "bitter coffee" types. In hindsight, the friends I have had that fit this description never fully displayed true friendship, and it is quite possible that I didn't show true friendship to them. Though Jesus offers the antithesis of this type of friendship, one of His twelve disciples fits the "bitter coffee" description to a "T."

The Bitter Cup Friend

📖 Read Luke 22:47–48. In what manner did Judas betray Jesus?

_____

_____

_____

_____

📖 Read Proverbs 21:10 in the margin. Describe how this proverb applies to the friendship of Jesus and Judas.

_____

_____

_____

📖 Now read Matthew 26:48–50. By what name did Jesus address Judas?

_____

_____

📖 Read Proverbs 12:20. Write your thoughts on how this proverb pertains to Judas and then to Jesus.

_____

_____

_____

I feel sure we all have felt betrayed by a "friend" at sometime in life. I don't believe you can make it through middle school or high school and not experience duplicity by a girlfriend or a boyfriend. Betrayal seems to hide in the lockers, cafeterias, and gyms just waiting to spring upon us in those vulnerable teen years.

(APPLY) Can you recall a time of feeling betrayed by someone close to your heart? Do you still feel the sting of hurt?

_____

_____

_____

Not only do these hurtful friends betray us, but they can also hurt us by leading us astray. In my early years, I was called upon to mentor a young woman about my age. As it turned out, our friendship instead of being uplifting and God-fearing turned into a disastrous road of sin. We were not wise in our decisions together. I watched with envy her ability to vomit up her food after she ate to keep her svelte shape. I attempted to become bulimic through her instruction.

Even more devastating was the criticism of our husbands that became the primary topic of conversation. We encouraged each other to live our lives to the fullest capability, with or without our husbands. We prodded one another into deeper and deeper sin. Eventually, we recognized our propensity for double trouble when we were together. The friendship ended, but not before we caused tremendous damage to our families and ourselves.

📖 Read Proverbs 2:12–15. Below, record next to each reference what can happen when a friendship takes the wrong course.

The Latte Friend:

"You use steel to sharpen steel, and one friend sharpens another."

Proverbs 27:17 (The Message)

"Wicked souls love to make trouble; they feel nothing for friends and neighbors."

Proverbs 21:10 (The Message)

Verse 12:

_____

Verse 13:

_____

Verse 14:

_____

Verse 15:

_____

Although, it may be necessary to break off a friendship, it doesn't mean that you become enemies. I remember a family member once asked me, "Don't you have any enemies?"

I hope not! The very thought scares me.

When I look at Jesus and Judas during the betrayal, I see Jesus display no bitterness nor anger. I see sorrow instead. Jesus fulfilled to the very end the words of the apostle Paul found in Romans 12:18, _"If it is possible, as far as it depends on you, live at peace with everyone."_

May that be said of every one of us who loves the Lord Jesus.

📖 Read Luke 9:57–62. Now apply Proverbs 19:4, 6 and relate these words to Jesus and His statements. How might some of His disciples and friends have reacted?

_____

_____

_____

_____

Today's Heart-Print
"Friends love through all kinds of weather." (Proverbs 17:17a; _The Message_)

Lord,

_____

_____

_____

_____

_____

_____

_____

_____

_____

_____

Extra Mile
CUP OF FRIENDSHIP

In closing our Day Four section, let's be grateful for our true friends. Let's thank them for their unique blend of friendship. Maybe we can send an occasional card, thanking them for their matchless places in our lives. Or better yet, we can call up girlfriends and invite them for coffee, our treat. Then we can relax for a while and enjoy a "cup of friendship."

Ask God to enrich your friendships and help you to become a better friend in each of them.

BEST FRIENDS FOREVER

A faithful friend is a strong defense: and he that hath found him, hath found a treasure—Apocrypha: Ecclesiasticus 6:14[9]

Do you know what BFF means? Neither did I. Recently, I spoke at a conference in California where a beautiful young woman worked the soundboard. I was desperate to have all the sessions recorded, so I could produce a good quality promotional CD.

Although, I try to record myself on a small digital recorder, it seems something always happens. The battery goes dead. The microphone doesn't work. Or more than likely, I forget to turn on the recorder. So as I said, I was desperate.

But this sweet servant of the Lord, smiled at me, crossed her fingers tightly in front of my face, and said, "I will be your BFF this weekend." Translated—Best Friend Forever.

As I pondered the acronym, BFF, I realized who that actually applies to— Jesus, of course. Today we are going to learn how to allow Jesus to become our best friend forever and discover how we can become friends with Him. Come on, let's cross our fingers tightly and speak the oath to learn how God can become our BFF.

📖 Read Proverbs 18:24b in the margin.

This proverb will constitute our primary verse for Day Five. Throughout Day Five we will examine how to have an intimate friendship with Jesus Christ. The word "friend" in this verse derives from the Hebrew word, *aheb*. Examine the Word Study sidebar concerning *aheb* and then write how you would apply what you learn about this word to your relationship with Jesus Christ.

_____

_____

_____

Commentator Matthew Henry wrote the following concerning Proverbs 18:24, "Christ Jesus never will forsake those who trust in and love him."[10] Let's take a look at what Jesus says in Matthew 28:20 and what His words mean to us here in the twenty-first century.

Please read Matthew 28:20. How long did Jesus say He would stay with us?

_____

_____

To cement this crucial promise, read the following verses and then place the correct reference to its corresponding statement. Read Deuteronomy 31:6, Psalm118:6, John 14:18, and Hebrews 13:5b.

"The LORD is with me; I will not be afraid."

My Heart's Cry:

Jesus, I want to be considered Your friend. Guide me in the manner so that I may increase the depth of our friendship, not just for now, but forever. In Your Precious name, Amen.

Word Study
FRIEND

The word "friend" in Proverbs 18:24 is translated from the Hebrew *aheb*, which can be defined in the following fashion: to love, desire, delight, like, be fond of, covet, be beloved, amiable, be a passionate lover. *Aheb* is often used in Scripture to describe the close attachment between parents and children. The term denotes a strong emotional attachment for and a desire to possess or be in the presence of the object of love. It implies an ardent and vehement inclination of the mind and a tenderness of affection at the same time. *Aheb* has the extensive sense of the English word "love."[11]

"But there is a friend who sticks closer than a brother."

Proverbs 18:24b

"Be strong and courageous. Do not be afraid or terrified because of them, for the LORD your God goes with you; he will never leave you nor forsake you."

"Never will I leave you; never will I forsake you."

"I will not leave you as orphans; I will come to you."

How would you apply these verses in contrast to Proverbs 19:4?

_____

_____

_____

_____

Do you trust that our God, Jesus Christ, will never leave us nor forsake us? No matter if we are wealthy or poor? If you do have this kind of trust, will you take a moment right now to thank God for His faithfulness? If you are lacking this level of trust, will you ask God to help you believe and trust in the above verses?

_____

_____

APPLY Let's get back to the subject of Jesus as our friend. How do you feel about God being *your* friend? Be honest!

_____

_____

_____

📖 OK, no matter what your answer was, let's take a look and see what Scripture states about being a friend of God. Read the following verses and name the friend of God mentioned.

Exodus 33:11 and Hebrews 11:24–28

_____

James 2:23

_____

📖 Abraham and Moses were God's friends. I want to peek at one more obscure person and see what it says about him. His name is Enoch. Please read Genesis 5:24 and Hebrews 11:5–6.

After reviewing these verses, it seems to me that Enoch was a friend of God, too. So what did Abraham, Moses, and Enoch do that enabled them to become friends with God?

Abraham (Exodus 33:11)

_____

Moses (Hebrews 11:24–28)

_____

Enoch (Genesis 5:24)

_____

📖 It doesn't sound very hard, does it? Abraham believed; Moses had faith; Enoch walked with God. So if we want to be friends with God, how can we believe, have faith, and walk with Him? Let's examine other verses to find the answer. Write down the instruction you find within these verses.

Romans 10:17

_____

John 14:21

_____

John 15:14

_____

📖 Now let's review Proverbs 2:1–8. Then journal your thoughts on how these proverbs apply to what Jesus said about his commandments, His love, and never forsaking us.

Verse 1

_____

_____

Verse 2

_____

_____

Verse 3

_____

_____

Verse 4

_____

_____

Verse 5

_____

_____

Verse 6

_____

_____

Verse 7

_____

_____

Verse 8

_____

_____

📖 Now let's review a few of the verses we have studied and consider if they apply to our friendship with Jesus. Read the following verses and then write the word "Christ" next to the references you believe apply to Christ.

Proverbs 17:17

Proverbs 18:1

Proverbs 19:4

Proverbs 22:11

Proverbs 26:18-19

Jesus is a friend who sticks by closer than a brother. He wants us to believe Him and to walk beside Him. Just as with any friendship, time must be spent building an intimate relationship with Christ. As the saying goes, time spent with Jesus is "time well spent."

📖 As we close out this lesson on friendship, I want us to quickly look at a few more verses that will deepen our relationship with God. Study the following verses and then note what you think each verse implies.

Mark 4:34b

_____

Mark 6:31

_____

Mark 9:2

_____

Time. We must spend time alone with Jesus. We have learned that Enoch walked with God. Is your time well spent? Today, as you journal in the "My Heart's Impression" section, use the vow to make Jesus your BFF—Best Friend Forever.

Today's Heart-Print
"Because God has said, "Never will I leave you; never will I forsake you."
(Hebrews 13:5b)

My Friend Jesus,

_____

_____

_____

_____

_____

_____

_____

Extra Mile
HARD SAYINGS

Read John 6. Jesus astonished people with His miracles. He fed over five thousand people with a mere five loaves of bread and two small fish. Because of what He provided by the miracles, the crowds, desired to make Him King. They were impressed by His feats, not with who He was.

But what happened when He spoke things that did not tickle their ears with what they wanted to hear?

Read John 2:24, 6:60–64.

How would Proverbs 19:4, 6 apply to Jesus and His friends?

Your Heart's Impression

Journal your thoughts about . . .

why friendship is important

_____

_____

_____

_____

what type of friends you desire to cultivate in your life

_____

_____

_____

_____

how you think of yourself as a friend

_____

_____

_____

_____

why you consider Jesus Christ to be your Best Friend Forever.

_____

_____

_____

_____

Tell Jesus what is in your heart after this lesson.

Jesus,

_____

_____

_____

_____

_____

_____

_____

_____

_____

1. http://quotes.prolix.nu/Authors/?C.S._Lewis

2. Frank S. Mead, *12,000 Religious Quotations*, (Grand Rapids, MI: Baker Book House), 1989. 156.

3. *Random House Webster's College Dictionary*. Random House, New York. 2001, pg. 735.

4. Matthew Henry, *Matthew Henry's Concise Commentary on the Whole Bible*. Thomas Nelson Publishers, Nashville. 1997, p. 280.

5. E. C. McKenzie, *14,000 Quips & Quotes For speakers, Writers, Editors, Preachers and Teachers*, Baker Book House. Grand Rapids, MI. 191.

6. John Cook, *The Book of Positive Quotations*. (New York: Grammercy Books, 1993), 109.

7. Edward K. Rowell & *Leadership Journal, 1001 Quotes, Illustrations, and Humorous Stories for Preachers, Teachers, & Writers* (Grand Rapids, MI: Baker Books, 1996), 73.

8. Mead, *12,000 Religious Quotations*, 155.

9. Ibid.

10. Matthew Henry, *Concise Commentary* in WORDsearch Bible software. CD-ROM, 2003.

11. Spiros Zodhiates, ed., *The Key Word Study Bible* (NIV) (Chattanooga, TN:AMG Publishers, 1996), Old Testament Lexical Aids, #170, 1501.

Heart-Print of Behaviors and Emotions

The true test of character is not how much we know how to do, but how we behave when we don't know what to do—John W. Holt

Eccentric people can make us laugh. They say and do funny things. Sometimes they appear foolish in our eyes. Have you ever appeared foolish to someone? I have.

At the beginning of the New Year, I determined that I would exercise more. A nice long walk each day became my goal. I like to walk with my two tiny Shih Tzu dogs, but they both have arthritis in their hind legs. I brainstormed a solution. I owned an old twin baby stroller. So, I plopped them in and off we went. I grabbed my sunglasses, and squinting at the bright sun, I quickly put on them on.

Another woman was walking her dog this particular morning. She stared at me a bit strangely. I grinned and said, "I know it looks ridiculous pushing these dogs in a baby stroller, but they can't walk very far." She nodded and then snatched her tiny Maltese dog. She strode away without another word.

After a three-mile walk, I came home quite pleased with my ingenuity. I lifted the dogs out of the twin stroller. I took off my sunglasses and placed them on the kitchen counter. To my surprise and horror, one of the dark lenses had fallen out. I realized how foolish I must have looked. Strolling two dogs in a baby stroller and staring out of sunglasses missing a lens. No wonder the woman grabbed her dog and high tailed it away from me.

Have you ever appeared foolish to someone?

I laughed until my sides ached. Although I looked and acted foolishly, it did no harm to anyone.

Unfortunately, some of our behaviors hurt others. On the other hand, many of our actions benefit people. This week we are going to study our behaviors. We'll look at the term folly. We'll investigate the destructive elements of anger, depression, and bitterness. We'll learn the profits of joy and love.

FOLLY OF FOOLS

That's the penalty we have to pay for our acts of foolishness—someone else always suffers for them—Alfred Sutro[2]

My Heart's Cry:

Father God, Grant me the wisdom to know when I am acting foolish. Allow me to learn to recognize when folly is knocking on the door of my mind. Show me the truth about my own folly and foolishness. Teach me how to resist them both. Amen.

Politicians never seem to admit their mistakes. They accuse and place blame on anyone else that might come in as a handy scapegoat. Although they have taken vows to behave with honesty and integrity, we continually read of lies and bribery taking place in all levels of government. Power, fame, and money often tempt them into foolish decisions that result in disastrous behaviors.

Today we are going to read about Balaam, a prophet in the Old Testament. He was much like our modern-day politicians. His fame at prophesying drew the attention of King Balak. Balak wanted Balaam to curse the Israelites, and so Balak bribed Balaam with rich rewards. But God emphatically told Balaam, "You must not put a curse on those people, because they are blessed" (Numbers 22:12). In modern-day English, God said to Balaam, "You've got to be kidding me. No way! I love them. They are My people."

Even so, Balaam kept searching for a way to curse the Israelites, but to no avail. The words that issued from his mouth pronounced blessings instead. But Balaam wanted the money. He acted in folly and connived to make his plan work. Let's discover how it turned out.

📖 Read Numbers 22:12–29. What would your thoughts and actions have been when the donkey talked?

_____

_____

_____

_____

It amazes me that Balaam didn't fall on his head in shock. But no, he actually answered the beast. What did he accuse the donkey of doing? (Verse 29)

_____

_____

📖 Now of course the donkey didn't make Balaam a fool. Balaam did it himself. Let's take a look at some proverbs to see what it takes to act like a fool. Read the following proverbs and then mark the statement next to it as true or false.

Proverbs 1:32	fools are complacent
Proverbs 10:21	fools die for lack of judgment
Proverbs 12:15	a fool listens to advice
Proverbs 12:16	a fool shows her annoyance
Proverbs 17:16	a fool desires wisdom
Proverbs 26:11	a fool learns from her mistakes

Well, I think Balaam fits the description for making himself into a fool. He didn't heed advice. Instead, he kept making the same stupid decisions to see if he could curse the Israelites. He beat his donkey in annoyance.

📖 Now compare Psalm 107:17 and Proverbs 10:23a. In your own words write down what these two verses tells us about fools.

_____

_____

_____

Fools are rebellious, and they find pleasure in their evil conduct. How would the story of Balaam apply to these concepts?

_____

_____

_____

The Bible reveals another fact about fools. Read in the margin Psalm 53:1a. From what you read in this verse, name another characteristic of a fool.

_____

_____

A fool will say there is no God. Have you ever met someone who mocked you for your belief in God? If yes, how did you respond?

_____

_____

_____

📖 Many times we come across as foolish to those who don't believe in God. Read the following Scripture passage and then jot down what appears to be foolishness to many people.

1 Corinthians 1:18–21

_____

_____

Do you remember a time when the death of Jesus appeared foolish to you?

_____

_____

I recall thinking the whole concept of the cross and forgiveness was about the silliest thing I had ever heard. Such a fool I was! Let's take a look at another type of fool that I emulated for years.

> *"The fool says in his heart, 'There is no God.'"*
> ## *Psalm 53:1a*

Doctrine
THE CROSS

Within the Roman Empire, death by crucifixion was rendered only to slaves, rebels, and the most notorious criminals who were not Roman citizens. It was against the law for a Roman to be executed by crucifixion.

The Jewish people of the time saw the practice shameful based on their recollection of Deuteronomy 21:22–23, "If a man guilty of a capital offense is put to death and his body is hung on a tree, you must not leave his body on the tree overnight. Be sure to bury him that same day, because anyone who is hung on a tree is under God's curse."

So for many living in the Roman Empire, including the majority of Jewish people, to believe that the Savior of the world, the Messiah, could die on a cross appeared ludicrous.

📖 Read Proverbs 19:3. What does this verse tell us happens in the heart of a fool when poor decisions bring disastrous results?

_____

_____

🛑 **APPLY** My heart raged at the Lord when my own poor choices proved disastrous in my life. What about you, can you describe a time when your heart raged against the Lord because of your own actions?

_____

_____

_____

📖 Gratefully, God is merciful to us. Read Psalm 85:8 and then paraphrase it.

_____

_____

It brings great comfort to know that when we listen to God, He will bring peace into our lives. Just this afternoon, my oldest son needed to make a life-changing decision. We prayed about it, and then I instructed him to listen carefully for God's answer. My son made his decision, and peace flowed in his mind.

What promise and warning is given in Psalm 85:8?

_____

_____

God does promise us peace, but He warns us not to return to our folly. So many times, we desire our own way, and we return to making poor decisions. That is the case with Balaam. Let's return for a moment to Balaam. How many times did he consider the proposition from King Balak (see Numbers 22:7–8, 15–19; 23:3, 15).

_____

_____

_____

📖 Scripture tells us that he considered it at least four times. He kept returning to his folly. Do you know why? Read 2 Peter 2:15 and Jude 11. What reason do these verses state for Balaam's continued folly?

_____

_____

_____

🛑 **APPLY** Obviously, he loved profit and the wages of wickedness. Would you have been tempted by King Balak's offers? If yes, explain. If no, name some areas where you might stumble into foolishness?

_____

_____

_____

Considering all that we studied today, explain how Isaiah 32:6 applies to Balaam?

_____

_____

Balaam spoke folly and his mind was busy with evil intentions. He practiced ungodliness and tried to bypass the Lord's will. He desired to curse the Israelites for profit rather than obey God's command. He made many foolish decisions. His donkey had more common sense than Balaam.

📖 I pray as we continue to study Proverbs, that we will make fewer foolish decisions. To close out Day One, please read Psalm 49:3–4. What do these verses advise us to do with a proverb?

_____

_____

In comparison, what does a fool do with a proverb according to Proverbs 26:7, 9?

_____

_____

We need to turn our ear to the wisdom of the Proverbs. However, the foolish person turns away from proverbial wisdom. Our words of wisdom to others become worthless when we act with folly.

🙏 Write a note to God. Tell Him what you thought about the lesson of Balaam. Ask Him to reveal to you areas of your own folly. Then write down Today's Heart-Print as a closing prayer.

Today's Heart-Print
I will listen to what God the Lord will say; he promises peace to his people, his saints but let them not return to folly. (Psalm 85:8)

Dear Lord,

_____

_____

_____

_____

_____

_____

_____

_____

_____

_____

_____

_____

> **"For the fool speaks folly, his mind is busy with evil: He practices ungodliness and spreads error concerning the Lord; the hungry he leaves empty and from the thirsty he withholds water."**
>
> **Isaiah 32:6**

POP GOES THE WEASEL

For every minute you are angry, you lose sixty seconds of happiness—
Author Unknown[3]

My heart broke today. The headlines in our local newspaper prominently displayed the words, "Unidentified Child Found Beaten to Death in Garbage Dumpster." The article went on to explain that a young girl, around the age of six, had been brutally beaten to death. No one claims to know her. The police were asking for help to identify her. The reward exceeded $50,000 to anyone aiding in the capture and conviction of her killer.

I understand anger. My oldest son was hyperactive to the extreme. As a young, high-strung mom, I became furious at times with some of his antics, though never to the point of harming him. I realized that when my anger popped up like a sneaky weasel, it was time to put my son in a time-out for awhile. I needed the break, and so did he for his own safety.

Today we live in a society of anger. Road rage rears its ugly head over minor traffic infractions. Small annoyances infuriate us. Corporations offer anger management courses to help us deal with our tempers.

Here in Day Two we are going to take our own anger management course as we open God's Word. The Bible has quite a lot to say about why we become angry and how we can deal with anger in a godly manner. Let's see what we can learn!

📖 Read Proverbs 27:4. Fill in the following blanks.

Anger is _____
And fury _____ _____
But who can stand before _____?

What does Proverbs 30:33 speak to us about anger?

_____

_____

"Anger is cruel and fury overwhelming, but who can stand before jealousy?"

Proverbs 27:4

📖 The result of stirring up anger is strife. Now let's study a biblical story of strife and anger. Please read Genesis 4:1–7.

How does verse 5 describe Cain?

_____

_____

What question did the Lord ask Cain?

_____

_____

What warning did God give to Cain?

_____

_____

📖 Now read Genesis 4:8. What happened after Cain ignored the Lord's caution?

_____

_____

📖 Reread Proverbs 27:4 and then apply it to Cain's story.

_____

_____

Cain's jealousy of Abel grew until it consumed him with the emotion of anger. The furious anger caused Cain to murder his own brother. It's hard for me to imagine that type of emotion and behavior. Yet, I read in the newspaper daily about family members who kill one another in a fit of rage. Unfortunately, the first type of murder recorded in the Bible, is now a commonplace occurrence.

📖 Read the following proverbs and then explain how they are applicable to Cain's anger:

Proverbs 29:11

_____

_____

Proverbs 29:22

_____

_____

APPLY Cain's jealous anger increased exponentially until he committed a horrible sin—the murder of his younger brother. He gave full vent to his anger instead of controlling it. Can you describe a time when your anger took control over your common sense?

_____

_____

📖 Read James 1:19–20. What does do these verses clearly express to us regarding anger?

_____

_____

_____

Anger in and of itself is not wrong. God created us to have this emotion. However, our anger should be against things that are wicked and unholy. The _Life Application Bible_ states it well,

> These verses speak of anger that erupts when our egos are bruised—'I am hurt'; 'My opinions are not being heard.' When injustice and sin occur, we should become angry because others are being hurt. But we should not become angry when we fail to win an argument or when we feel offended or neglected. Selfish anger never helps anybody.[5]

We should not use our anger to harm others in any way. I come from a family that took pride in their anger. My maiden name is Shurtliff. We often

"Anger is one letter short of danger."

—Author Unknown[4]

bragged about having a "Shurtliff fit." In other words, a temper tantrum over someone or something.

I remember one time I was so angry at my computer. The seething rage in me felt uncontrollable. I yelled, "I am throwing this stupid computer out in the street." My husband responded, "If you do, it will be your last computer." Maybe it was time for me to be in "time out." Fortunately, I restrained myself from doing something so foolish. If we are completely honest, we all can list occasions where anger brought us to the point of meltdown.

APPLY Will you list a few inanimate objects that make your temper flare-up?

_____

_____

📖 Read Proverbs 14:17a in the margin.

Have you ever done something foolish (like throw a computer) due to your quick temper?

_____

_____

What was the end result?

_____

_____

Although inanimate items can make us lose our tempers, people usually are the primary cause.

📖 Read the following proverbs and note *who* seems to ignite anger within us?

Proverbs 14:21a

_____

_____

Proverbs 17:1

_____

_____

Proverbs 22:10

_____

_____

Proverbs 26:17

_____

_____

Proverbs 26:18

_____

_____

"A quick-tempered man does foolish things."

Proverbs 14:17a

I'll bet you have encountered all kinds of people like the ones described in these proverbs. Probably each of us has behaved like these people on some occasion.

APPLY Please circle the following behaviors if you know a person who acted in such a manner and filled you with outrage. And then place a check beside the behaviors where you have angered another person.

mocker and sarcasm   reckless actions

meddler and busybody   caused strife in the family

angered a neighbor   insulted someone

It seems many situations can raise our ire. Match the following proverbs with the correlating action.

Proverbs 12:16   greed

Proverbs 16:28   stirs up dissension

Proverbs 25:23   rages and scoffs

Proverbs 27:3   provocation

Proverbs 28:25   sly tongue

Proverbs 29:9   show annoyance quickly

📖 Well, as you can see all sorts of people, things, and actions can provoke us. Now let's determine how we can best handle our anger when we feel it bubbling up. Read the following verses and write the anger management technique outlined in each verse next to the reference:

Proverbs 15:18

_____

_____

Proverbs 17:14

_____

_____

Proverbs 26:20

_____

_____

Proverbs 29:11

_____

_____

We all feel anger at times. So when the weasel of anger pops up its ugly head, perhaps we should drop the matter for a while at least. Often, the more we discuss a situation with others when our "dander is up" the less likely we will be able to resolve the issue. We need to remember the adage that cooler heads prevail. When we follow these biblical solutions, usually our anger dissipates, and suitable resolutions are reached.

📖 Let's look at another important solution to anger. Please write what Ephesians 4:26 speaks to you.

_____

_____

Scripture is clear that we should not allow anger to fester overnight. The danger in allowing our anger to linger is that resentment and bitterness tend to build until a small quarrel turns into a bitter battle.

📖 Now let's look at a few New Testament verses as we close Day Two. Read the following verses and fill-in the blanks.

Colossians 3:8

_"But now you must rid yourselves of all such things as these: _____, _____, _____, _____, and filthy language from your lips."_

Romans 12:18

_"If it is possible, as far as it _____ _____ _____, live at _____ with everyone."_

As Christians we need to pursue righteous living. We should rid our lives of anger, rage, malice, and slander. Our goal should be to live in peace with everyone whenever it's within our control.

Today's Heart-Print
" 'In your anger do not sin': Do not let the sun go down while you are still angry" (Ephesians 4:26)

Write a personal prayer to God by rewording Colossians 3:8, and Romans 12:8. (These are the verses we just filled in the blanks.)

Lord God,

_____

_____

_____

_____

_____

_____

_____

> **"In your anger do not sin: Do not let the sun go down while you are still angry."**
>
> **Ephesians 4:26**

Behaviors & Emotions

DAY THREE

TWIN SISTERS

The greatest thing a man can do for his heavenly Father is to be kind to some of His other children—Henry Drummond[6]

My sister-in-law birthed identical twin boys. Our family's exhilaration over the twin siblings increased our time with each other. Suddenly, we visited more often. We called frequently and dashed to hold the little guys whenever opportunities arose.

Although the boys looked identical, little differences began to display themselves. One baby listened quietly. The other loved to gurgle, coo, and babble. One crawled across the carpet. The other boy rolled to grab the bottle. So much alike, yet so different. We love them both just the same though.

📖 Today we are going to study behaviors that often seem identical, yet are slightly dissimilar. And to live godly lives we desperately need both of them. Read the following verses and see if you can discover two similar traits of godly conduct.

1 Corinthians 13:4
2 Corinthians 6:6
Galatians 5:22
Colossians 3:12

Did you discover that kindness and patience were linked together in each verse? Sometimes, as in Galatians 5:22, the two words sit right next to each other. This intertwined correlation of patience and kindness speaks directly to us. We should strive to understand and develop both of these behaviors in our daily lives.

Before we jump into some proverbs, let's take a moment to investigate the terms *kind* and *patient*. Without looking at a dictionary, please define what they suggest to you.

"kind" or "kindness"

_____

_____

"patient" or "patience"

_____

_____

Now lets delve into the original Greek language for a better comprehension of why these two English words were chosen by our translators. Read both Word Study sidebars in the margin, then compare and contrast them with how you defined *kind* and *patient*.

_____

_____

_____

For myself, I discovered that kindness involves action. I must be willing to assist someone. For patience, I learned that it certainly involves long-suffering. That means sometimes it's going to hurt me when I make the decision to be patient.

And have you ever considered that there are two different types of patience?

📖 Read the following two verses. Note what each denotes have patience with.

"Be completely humble and gentle; be patient, bearing with one another in love." (Ephesians 4:2 NIV)

_____

_____

My Heart's Cry:
Oh Jesus, send Your Holy Spirit to enable me to be kind and patient with others. Grant me a double portion of kindness, so that the light of Your love may shine in this dark world. Amen.

"Love is patient, love is kind. It does not envy, it does not boast, it is not proud."

1 Corinthians 13:4

"We can rejoice, too, when we run into problems and trials, for we know that they are good for us—they help us learn to be patient." (Romans 5:3; LB)

_____

_____

Word Study
PATIENCE

In Galatians 5:22, the word "patience" is translated from the Greek *makrothumia*, meaning long-suffering, to suffer long, be long-suffering, as opposed to showing hasty anger or punishment. *Makrothumia* also means "to forbear, to endure patiently as opposed to losing faith or giving up." It can also mean "to tarry, delay." *Makrothumia* is translated "patient" in 1 Corinthians 13:4. In Ephesians 4:2, *makrothumia* is used to describe one exercising understanding and patience with others.[7]

One type of patience concerns people, while the other deals with circumstances. Which is more difficult for you to exhibit—patience with people or circumstances? Why?

_____

_____

_____

I know for myself, people test my patience more than annoying circumstances do. I believe our Day Three examination of Proverbs will reinforce this notion.

Now lets get into some proverbs and learn more about the principles of patience and kindness—two characteristics presented in the New Testament as evidences of the fruit of the Holy Spirit (see Galatians 5:22).

📖 Read the following proverbs. Mark a "P" if the term *patience* applies to people or a "C" if it applies to annoying circumstances in the verse. Then write the benefit noted for those who display patience.

Proverbs 14:29

_____

Proverbs 15:18b

_____

Proverbs 16:32

_____

Proverbs 19:11

_____

Proverbs 25:15

_____

Doctrine
KINDNESS

In Galatians 5:22, the word "kindness" comes from the Greek word *chrestotes* (goodness, excellence, uprightness). A variant of this word (*chresteuomai*) is translated "kind" in 1 Corinthians 13:4. In this verse another effective translation of *chresteuomai* is "useful." *Chresteuomai* refers to one who is kind, obliging, or willing to help or assist.[8] When we love someone, we will be kind to them and willing to aid and assist them.

📖 Now let's take a peek at *kindness*. Match the blessings of being kind with the correct proverb.

Proverbs 11:17	a kind word cheers an anxious heart
Proverbs 12:25	the Lord will reward kindness to the poor
Proverbs 14:21	being kind to the needy honors God
Proverbs 14:31	a kind man benefits himself
Proverbs 19:17	blessed is the one who is kind to the needy

📖 Certainly blessings abound for those who model kindness and patience. Of course, God is the ultimate model for both. Read the following scriptures and then note the reason why God shows patience and kindness.

Jeremiah 31:3

_____

Romans 2:4

_____

Titus 3:4

_____

2 Peter 3:9

_____

2 Peter 3:15

_____

God's kindness and patience lead us to repentance. Read the following quote in the margin by Frederick W. Faber. Next, write down the reason why this quote is true when people are kind with one another. If possible, give an example of someone accepting Jesus Christ as a result of another person's modeling God's patience and kindness.

📖 As we read, part of the fruit of the Holy Spirit is patience and kindness. Read Galatians 5:25 and then fill-in the blanks.

_"Since we _____ by the _____, let us _____ in _____ with the Spirit."_

APPLY Let's end Day Three by making a list of people whom we need to show more kindness or patience to in our lives.

_____

_____

🙏 Ask God to develop these qualities in you through the power of His son Jesus and the Holy Spirit. Pray that you learn to keep in step with the Holy Spirit when you deal with people who try your kindness and patience. Tell God how thankful you are for Christ's kindness and patience, which led to your own redemption.

Today's Heart-Print
"Love is patient, love is kind" (1 Corinthians 13:4)

Lord Jesus,

_____

_____

_____

_____

_____

> **"Kindness converted more sinners than zeal, eloquence, or learning."**
>
> **—Frederick W. Faber**[9]

JOY TO THE WORLD

Joy is the echo of God's life within us—Joseph Marmion[10]

My Heart's Cry:

Lord Jesus, awake my soul to true joy. Teach me to experience joy regardless of my day-to-day state of affairs. I thank You that You are my joy giver. In Your name, Amen.

A few years ago I spoke to a young mother's group during the festive Christmas season. In relation to the joy and happiness associated with Christmas, I presented my opinion that happiness and joy are two different emotions. The young women listened as their babies fidgeted. One mom filed her manicured nails and yawned. Tear's glistened in another mommy's eyes as I told them that happiness comes and goes in quick sessions based on the comfort of our circumstances. Joy lingers deep in our souls regardless of life's difficulties. True joy comes from deep within, and its basis is discovered in the joy of knowing Jesus.

The teary-eyed woman thanked me profusely. She told me how she would pursue joy instead of straining for happiness while preparing for Christmas. Then I overheard the lovely manicured lady say, "Well, a new cashmere sweater would bring me more joy than Jesus could." She walked away searching for joy in an inanimate object that would soon lose its compelling luster.

Other divergent reactions to the message of pursuing joy rather than happiness occurred that day. Today as we study Scripture, I pray that we find joy beyond the measure of this world's standards. Before we look at Proverbs, I want to look at a few New Testament verses about true joy. Ready?

📖 Read the following verses and make a note of what they tell us about Jesus' joy.

Luke 10:21

_____

Hebrews 1:8–9

_____

Hebrews 12:2

_____

Jesus has been anointed and is full of joy. He knows all about rejoicing. He suffered the horror of crucifixion for the joy set before Him. What was that joy? Christ's joy came in knowing that He made salvation and eternal life possible for us. What did Jesus tell His disciples to rejoice about in Luke 10:20?

_____

_____

_____

APPLY How often do you rejoice in your priceless salvation through the blood of Jesus Christ? Will you take a moment to rejoice and write Christ a note of thanksgiving?

_____

_____

📖 Let's see where else we can find joy in our lives. Read the following proverbs and then fill in the blanks.

Proverbs 10:1   *"A _____ _____ bring joy to his father."*

Proverbs 15:23   *"A man finds joy in giving an _____."*

Proverbs 15:30   *"A _____ brings joy to the heart."*

Proverbs 27:9a   *"_____ and _____ bring joy to the heart."*

When I sit down for my devotional times, I like to burn fragrant candles. It lifts my soul and spirit. A shout for joy wants to spring from my heart when I come up with an apt answer, as usually I am not that good at thinking on my feet. I would never make the debate team, but occasionally, something wise spouts from my mouth surprising me and amazing others. Yes, these things are cause for joyful moments in my life. But nothing brings more joy to my heart than when one of my children makes a wise decision.

🛑 **APPLY** Will you list a few things that bring joy to your spirit and soul?

_____

_____

Let's take a quick look at things that might bring us happiness, even though that happiness may be short lived.

📖 Mark "True" next to any of the following Scripture passages that convey the ability to bring happiness. Under those you think are indicative of some form of happiness, give a "ballpark figure" of the amount of time you think such happiness could last.

Ecclesiastes 5:19–20

_____

Ecclesiastes 7:14

_____

Proverbs 10:2a

_____

Proverbs 11:4

_____

Proverbs 21:6

_____

Proverbs 22:9

_____

Proverbs 27:2

_____

Some things may bring happiness, but often the happiness is short-lived. Jonah, the Old Testament prophet, experienced short-term happiness. Read Jonah 4:6–8. What made Jonah happy? What made him angry?

Put Yourself in Their Shoes
JONAH

Jonah's happiness fluctuated based on his current circumstances. Read the Book of Jonah. Then make a list of his fluctuating emotions and behaviors. Ponder what your own emotions and behaviors might have been had you been in his situation.

_____

_____

_____

📖 How could Proverbs 27:1 apply to Jonah and the vine?

_____

_____

We never know what the future holds. What might bring happiness and comfort in life today could be gone tomorrow. Jonah based his happiness on his temporal circumstances. However, when God withered the vine, Jonah's happiness turned to anger.

Take a moment to ponder what might bring you short-term happiness. Then consider what brings you lasting joy.

	Happiness	Joy
1.	_____	_____
2.	_____	_____
3.	_____	_____
4.	_____	_____
5.	_____	_____

A nice dinner out with my husband brings me great happiness. And I suppose a cashmere sweater on a chilly winter day might make me happy, too. However, the love of my husband, time with my children, and visits with my extended family cause great joy to well up inside of me.

APPLY I see a common denominator to my joy: time spent with people I love. Can you find a common denominator within your list of joys?

_____

_____

_____

"But the righteous sings and rejoices."

Proverbs 29:6b
(NASB)

📖 Let's read why we can experience long-lasting joy. Please read Proverbs 29:6b in the margin.

Now study Romans 4:21–25. According to these verses, how do we become righteous? What did Jesus do for us?

_____

_____

📖 Now reread Hebrews 12:2. Please place your name in the blank space for this verse below and make it personal.

_"Let _____ fix her eyes on Jesus the author and perfecter of her faith, who for the joy set before him endured the cross, scorning its shame and sat down at the right hand of God."_

📖 Jesus knew the joy that awaited Him when He sat down at the right hand of God. What does this mean for us? Read the following verses and personalize them according to the Hebrews 12:2 example above.

John 15:10–11

"If _____ obey my commands, _____ will remain in my love, just as I have obeyed my Father's commands and remain in his love. I have told _____ this so that my joy may be in _____ and that _____ joy may be complete."

John 16:24b

"Ask and _____ will receive and _____ joy will be complete."

📖 What did Jesus pray for us in John 17:13?

_____

_____

Jesus was filled with joy. He desires for joy to flood our souls. He prayed for a full measure of joy to flood our souls. If we are not joy-filled, we should ask Him to accept the joy of the righteous, because by His death on the cross we have become righteous.

📖 How would this verse apply to Proverbs 10:28 and 11:10?

_____

_____

APPLY As we finish Day Four, please read 1 Peter 1:8. Define what this verse means to you and your relationship with the Lord Jesus Christ.

_____

_____

_____

_____

Today's Heart-Print
"The prospect of the righteous is joy, but the hopes of the wicked come to nothing"
(Proverbs 10:28)

Let's thank Jesus our joy giver for what He has done for us. Try to express your glorious joy in Him.

My Jesus,

_____

_____

_____

_____

_____

_____

_____

_____

"Let us fix our eyes on Jesus, the author and perfecter of our faith, who for the joy set before him endured the cross, scorning its shame, and sat down at the right hand of the throne of God."

Hebrews 12:2

MENTAL MENAGERIE

You don't get to choose how you're going to die. You can only decide how you're going to live.—Joan Baez[11]

ecision, decisions, decisions. Life is full of choices. Think about the following people who made history with their judgment calls

Pilate: The Crucifixion of Christ

President Harry Truman: The Atomic Bomb

Rosa Parks: Civil Rights

George W. Bush: The War in Iraq

For most of us, we will not need to make decisions that change the course of our nation or our world. However, we make choices that affect our lives and others around us. The Book of Proverbs gives abounding advice on a host of topics that will help us in our walk of life.

📖 Let's grab as much wisdom as we can from Proverbs as we journey through Day Five. Read Proverbs 12:15. What instruction does this proverb give to us?

_____

_____

_____

📖 This proverb counsels us to listen to advice. There are several ways we can receive advice, such as through our spouses, our friends, pastoral counsel, and of course God's Word. Read the following proverbs and note how they concur to Proverbs 12:15.

Proverbs 11:14

_____

Proverbs 15:22

_____

Proverbs 20:18

_____

All of these proverbs strongly suggest we get advice and counsel before making decisions. Earlier in this study, I mentioned the decision of Pilate to cave into political pressure and order Christ to be crucified. Let's look at the counsel he sought.

📖 Read the following verses and then list the different people who gave advice to Pilate. Jot down examples of people who gave wise counsel. Then note who directed Pilate to make his final decision.

Luke 22:66—23:4

_____

_____

Luke 23:6–16

_____

_____

John 18:33–38

_____

_____

John 19:6–8

_____

_____

Matthew 27:19

_____

_____

How does Proverbs 12:5 apply to Pilate's situation?

_____

_____

APPLY Please note a few times when you heeded godly counsel from someone. How did things turn out?

_____

_____

_____

The advice of wicked people will lead others astray. Can you relate? Do you recall a time when heeding poor advice proved to be disastrous in your life? What was the result?

_____

_____

_____

Now let's look at the flipside, can you think of times when you gave godly advice or perhaps offered poor suggestions? What happened?

_____

_____

_____

📖 Good advice is divinely sent. However, poor recommendations can destroy relationships, finances, and a myriad of other things. Proverbs 13 overflows with admonitions. How does each of the following verses pertain to receiving or giving advice?

Verse 10

_____

My Heart's Cry:

Lord God, my thoughts run erratic paths. Daily decisions overwhelm me. Remind me to seek You when difficult choices confront me. Allow my thoughts to be centered on You and promises in Your Word. In Jesus' name, Amen.

"The way of a fool seems right to him, but a wise man listens to advice."

Proverbs 12:15

_____

Verse 14

_____

Verse 16

_____

Verse 17

_____

Verse 20

_____

Did You Know?

THE TRIALS OF JESUS

Jesus had six trials before His crucifixion. The Jewish phases of Jesus' trial consisted of an appearance before Annas (the father-in-law of Caiaphas), Caiaphas (the high priest), and then the Sanhedrin, which consisted of Jewish religious leaders.

The Roman trial of Jesus also had three phases: first, Christ's appearance before Pilate the Roman Procurator of Judea, then an appearance before Herod Antipas, the Roman appointed "king" of the Jewish people, and then a final appearance before Pilate. Between the two judicial systems the six trials concluded with a sentence of death for Jesus.

These verses advise us to listen to wise advice and to understand that poor counsel has the potential to destroy us. Peer pressure from others can lead us to a string of poor choices, bad habits, and strongholds of addictions.

For example, my friend's nephew was an honor roll student and superb athlete. However, he made an initial poor choice to use drugs with the urging of his friends. It was not long until the talented young man succumbed to a drug addiction.

With every bad habit or addiction an initial choice is made. Whether it is the first peek at pornography, the fib for the compulsive liar, or the sip of alcohol for the drunk, it all begins with the first poor decision. For many people, addictions become devices to escape from the difficulty and pain in their lives.

Read Proverbs 23:29–35. Underline the phrases that point to escapism through an addiction. Then circle any warning you discover in these verses.

"Who has woe? Who has sorrow? Who has strife? Who has complaints? Who has needless bruises? Who has bloodshot eyes? Those who linger over wine, who go to sample bowls of mixed wine. Do not gaze at wine when it is red, when it sparkles in the cup, when it goes down smoothly! In the end it bites like a snakeand poisons like a viper. Your eyes will see strange sights and your mind imagine confusing things. You will be like one sleeping on the high seas,lying on top of the rigging. 'They hit me,' you will say, 'but I'm not hurt!' They beat me, but I don't feel it! When will I wake up so I can find another drink?" (Proverbs 23:29–35)

 My heart rends at the last line, "When will I wake up so I can find another drink?" The mental anguish speaks clearly. Can you think of people you know that seek comfort through addictions? If yes, what are their addictions?

_____

_____

_____

Please match the following proverbs with the phrase concerning possible addictions, bad habits, or sin.

Proverbs 5:1–6   gluttony
Proverbs 14:5   lying
Proverbs 20:1   adultery
Proverbs 23:20–21   alcoholism
Proverbs 23:26–28   promiscuous behavior, adultery

📖 Thankfully, we can break free from these behaviors or any others that
   bind us. What promises do we find in the following New Testament
   verses concerning freedom from poor choices and addictions?

Luke 4:14–21

_____

_____

_____

Galatians 5:1

_____

_____

_____

Jesus Christ came to free us. It is within His strength that we can be set free.
If you are struggling with an addiction, please seek godly counsel. The pastoral staff of your church can offer assistance, even if it is nothing more than
directing you to godly professional counselors that live and work your area.

Hopefully, my friend's son will stay clean and sober from his drug
addiction. Let's take a moment to pray for someone, perhaps ourselves, who requires freedom from bad habits and addictions. Let's
ask the Father to grant us wise advisors in all of our decisions. Let's
allow Jesus to set us free of the things that so easily entangle us (see
Hebrews 12:1).

_____

_____

_____

_____

> "The plans of the righteous are just, but the advice of the wicked is deceitful."
>
> **Proverbs 12:5**

Today's Heart-Print
The plans of the righteous are just, but the advice of the wicked is deceitful.
(Proverbs 12:5)

Your Heart's Impression

Journal your thoughts about . . .

how to avoid foolish behaviors:

_____

_____

_____

making peace with others in your life:

_____

_____

_____

your need for more kindness and patience:

_____

_____

_____

how you will find godly counsel for difficult decisions in your life:

_____

_____

_____

Tell the Lord God what is in your heart after this week's lesson.
Lord God,

_____

_____

_____

_____

_____

_____

_____

_____

_____

_____

1. John Cook, *The Book of Positive Quotations* (New York: Grammercy Books, 1993), 420.

2. http://www.quotationsbook.com/authors/7065/Alfred_Sutro.

3. E. C. McKenzie, *14,000 Quips & Quotes For Speakers, Writers, Editors, Preachers and Teachers* (Grand Rapids, MI: Baker Book House), 553.

4. Ibid., 23.

5. *Life Application Bible* (Wheaton, IL: Tyndale House, 1991). 2246.

6. Frank S. Mead, *12,000 Religious Quotations* (Grand Rapids, MI: Baker Book House, 1989), 264.

7. Spiros Zodhiates, Th.D., *The Complete Word Study Dictionary New Testament* (Chattanooga, TN: AMG Publishers, 1992), 939, 3114.

8. Ibid., 1481, 5541.

9. http://www.wisdomquotes.com/002506.html

10. Mead, *12,000 Religious Quotations*, 258.

11. Cook, *The Book of Positive Quotations,* 311.

LESSON SIX

Heart-Print of Motherhood

A really good parent is a provider, a counselor, an advisor, and when necessary, a disciplinarian—Anonymous[1]

First, I want to assure you even if you are not a mom in the strictest sense of the word, this week's lessons will still apply to you. We will study not only parenting biological or adopted children, but also our spiritual children. In God's parental economy, children come in all shapes, sizes, and ages. His view of parenthood differs from our ordinary understanding. If you do not have children, apply the parts of this lesson to women whom you influence in your life.

Although I gave birth to two sons, God has granted me amazing daughters-in-laws. I refer to them as my "daughters-in-love." In addition, His blessings include numerous spiritual daughters of faith. As we proceed with this week's lesson, keep in mind the different areas where you may be considered a "mother in the faith." Perhaps you teach Sunday school or aid in the youth group? Are you an aunt to someone? Or could you be the "nice lady" down the street who allows kids to play ball in her yard and bakes fluffy sugar cookies?

Parenting and mentoring anyone is difficult. However because we are not given a parenting how-to-manual, most parental skills are learned by trial and error. (I refer to my eldest son as "my experimental child.") Fortunately, the Proverbs grant us insight into godly ways to parent. They give us recommendations, suggestions, and concrete instructions on how we should raise our children. This week's lesson will give us pointers on how to instruct, discipline, and raise faithful children whether they are our own kids or perhaps spiritual children that God allows us to "parent" for a season.

> *Even if you are not a mom in the strictest sense of the word, this week's lesson will still apply to you.*

A QUIVER FULL OF BLESSINGS

No man is poor who has a godly mother—Abraham Lincoln[2]

My Heart's Cry:

Dear Father, teach me to be a better mother. Help me to mentor others so that You are glorified by their lives. In Jesus' name, Amen.

My sister-in-law recently delivered identical twin boys. Her little two-year old guy can hardly wait until his baby brothers are big enough to play. She laughs at the thought of having three sons. Already each of the little boys has their own distinct personality. One is rambunctious, one a snuggler, and the other is just a laid-back dude who watches the others as if to say, "Hey chill out!" As each of them grows, my dear sister-in-law will need to know how to teach and discipline each one in their own way.

For myself, my two sons are as different as night and day. One son needed excitement and activity to learn. My younger introverted son preferred less noise and more structure. Trying to find a creative balance in parenting can be difficult. I have heard said, "Your first child is experimental!"

But God has given us certain concepts on how to raise children. Here in Day One, we are going to look at the blessings of having children whether they are biological, adopted, or spiritual children.

Read Psalm 127:3–5. What do these verses state about the blessings and advantages of children?

_____

_____

Children are a heritage from the Lord. We are blessed when our lives are full of children. And when trouble arises, they can help us contend with our problems. So let's look at the variety of children that could come into our lives.

Read the following verses and note what type of birth is mentioned:

Proverbs 23:25

_____

James 1:18

_____

"For God so loved the world that he gave his one and only Son, that whoever believes in him shall not perish but have eternal life."

John 3:16

Of course, we women are blessed (or cursed depending how you look at it) with the ability to give birth. But James tells us God chose to "give us birth through the word that we might be a kind of first fruits of all he created." In other words, He allows us to accept a spiritual rebirth. Read what Jesus said in John 3:1–16. Describe what these verses mean to you.

_____

_____

_____

Jesus explained to Nicodemus that he must be born not only of a woman, but that he must be born again in the Spirit. He goes on to explain with the familiar verses of John 3:16 that by accepting Christ Jesus as your Lord, then you will be born of the Spirit and have eternal life.

📖 Let's review a few various descriptions of children found in the New Testament. Note the term used to describe children and jot down if they are physical or spiritual.

Mark 10:13–16

_____

1 Corinthians 3:1

_____

Galatians 3:26

_____

Ephesians 1:5

_____

Jesus loved children. Did you discover that we are considered children regardless of our age? And just as the apostle Paul described himself as a parent to others of the faith, we can become mothers of faith to others.

📖 Read Luke 10:17–21. Examine what Jesus said about little children and describe how it could apply to new believers.

_____

_____

_____

Jesus praised the Father for revealing things of the Kingdom to "little children." In Mark 10, He admonishes His disciples who viewed certain children flocking to Jesus as bothersome and unimportant.

🛑 APPLY Please list five people whom would consider *you* as a mother figure in their life. What is your relationship to each of these individuals?

1.

_____

2.

_____

3.

_____

4.

_____

5.

_____

📖 Read the following proverbs and note how the reader is addressed. Also, what theme of action do these verses promote?

Extra Mile
LUKE 10

Read Luke 10. List the instructions that Jesus gave to the seventy-two. Journal your thoughts about Jesus' words in verses 2, 21–23. How would these verses apply to Psalm 127:3–5?

Proverbs 1:8

_____

Proverbs 5:1

_____

Proverbs 4:10

_____

Proverbs 4:20

_____

"Listen, my son, to your father's instruction and do not forsake your mother's teaching."

Proverbs 1:8

Each of these proverbs addresses the reader as *"my son."* Each proverb then advises the actions of listening to instruction. Let's go back for a moment to the people who look to you as a mother figure in their lives. What type of instruction or advice do you give them? For example, if it is your kids, do you teach them about the dangers of talking to strangers? Are you modeling manners and civility to others? Maybe you teach a Bible study to the "children" in your life?

Our families may consist of parents, children, grandparents, aunts, uncles, and numerous cousins. Or maybe your family consists of friends. Perhaps you mentor someone whom you love dearly. Regardless whom you consider as your family, high-quality relationships do not happen by coincidence. They result from a concentrated effort to teach and learn godly principles. As we see the results of our maternal teachings accepted and acted upon, we are blessed. As Jesus said, *"The harvest is plentiful, but the workers are few. Ask the Lord of the harvest, therefore, to send out workers into his harvest field"* (Luke 10:2).

Today, whether you have toddlers pulling at your pants, a neighbor who needs a listening ear, or a teenager who seems to ignore your advice, will you take a few moments and pray for them? Ask God to show you how to become a better mother and to fill your quiver full of blessed children.

Today's Heart-Print
May your father and mother be glad; may she who gave you birth rejoice!
(Proverbs 23:25)

Father God,

_____

_____

_____

_____

_____

_____

_____

_____

_____

A Trust is Given

All I am my mother made me—John Quincy Adams[3]

I sat in the doctor's office with my seventeen-year-old son. A moment of *déjà vu* struck me as he opened supply drawers. He scooted across the white paper on the examination table. His feet kicked and banged against the metal trays.

Suddenly, laughter overwhelmed me. When Jeremy was a five-year-old, he acted out the same behaviors as I scrambled to prevent destruction of the exam room. "Yes, the doctor diagnosed, he is definitely hyperactive with attention-deficit disorder." An A.D.H.D. kid was God's choice for me to parent. "Well, it sure wouldn't be dull," I thought.

Although never dull, many times I wanted to throw my hands in the air and quit the task of parenting. Motherhood entails joy and heartache. It means lack of sleep, lack of being understood, and a mountain of self-sacrifice. To parent or mentor someone requires a heart of commitment.

So in Day Two, we are going to explore the concept of our children as treasures entrusted to us for a season. Although ultimately they belong to God, He allows us the honor of training our children for approximately eighteen years or more. We'll reinforce the idea that parenting isn't always easy, but it's worth the effort.

📖 Let's start with a heart-rending story of motherhood. Please read 1 Kings 3:16–28.

How did the king decide who was the true mother of the child?

_____

_____

Why did the actual mother react as she did?

_____

_____

King Solomon recognized the sacrificial heart of the rightful mother. She would rather give up the child than to see him come to harm. He then granted the living child to this woman who demonstrated compassion for her child.

I believe Solomon recognized the true love of a parent, because he had experienced this kind of love from his parents.

📖 Read Proverbs 4:1–4.

What do you discover about Solomon in these verses?

_____

_____

_____

My Heart's Cry:

Lord, I am honored to be given the privilege of raising my children. Plus, You have entrusted a few of Your children for me to guide in their faith walk. Today, I ask Your guidance in this challenging responsibility. Remind me to diligently pray and seek Your assistance as I parent those entrusted to me. In Your name, Amen.

Solomon's father taught him from his lap the words of wisdom. He mentions that he was the only child of his mother. The words *"only child,"* can also be translated as "one especially beloved."[4] Can't you just hear the nostalgic tone in these verses? Solomon understood a parent's love, because he was loved by his own parents.

Read the following verses and note how a mother's love is described.

Isaiah 49:15

_____

Isaiah 66:13

_____

1 Thessalonians 2:7

_____

Solomon's parents trained him from a very young age to listen and obey the commands of God. Read the following proverbs and note the common theme in each one.

Proverbs 2:1

_____

Proverbs 3:1

_____

Proverbs 4:10

_____

Proverbs 4:20

_____

Proverbs 5:1

_____

Proverbs 5:7

_____

Repeatedly we read words such as "listen to me." (By the way, the word *"son"* or *"sons"* in these proverbs can be translated as "child" or "children.") From these passages, we see that Solomon received training and instruction from his parents.

In the margin, please read Proverbs 22:6. At first glance, what does this proverb seem to promise?

_____

_____

"Train a child in the way he should go, and when he is old he will not turn from it."

Proverbs 22:6

Proverbs 22:6 is one of most frequently quoted of the Proverbs. At first glance, it seems to say that if we train our children correctly, they will surely be obedient, godly adults. Do I hear parental groans from those of us who have rebellious children? Before you begin to feel guilty, we need to take a closer look at how the total concept of this verse should be understood. We are going to look at two slightly different commentaries on this verse.

The first comes from *Hard Sayings of the Bible*. Concerning Proverbs 22:6, it states,

> The statement is called a proverb, not a promise. Many godly parents have raised their children in ways that were genuinely considerate of the children's own individuality and the high calling of God, yet the children have become rebellious and wicked.
>
> There is, however, the general principle that sets the standard for the majority. This principle urges parents to give special and detailed care with the awesome task of rearing children so that the children may continue in that path long after the lessons have ceased.[5]

The *Hebrew-Greek Key Study Bible* offers another interpretation. The explanatory notes for Proverbs 22:6 make the following observations,

> The quality of training which the child receives is of critical concern. Parents should not assume that simply bringing their children up in a moral atmosphere is all that is needed. The primary goal in training up a child is that he is educated in the knowledge of God, but he should also be provided with a thorough preparation for life in general. When a child does choose to rebel and lead a corrupt life, it is often the parents who have failed in teaching or setting an example. It must be recognized, however, that there will be instances when the parents have done their best to train a child correctly, yet he will choose to reject the instruction he has received and go his own way.[6]

Do you see that we are responsible for our children, yet they are also responsible for their own decisions in life?

I would like to try to explain how I see this concept of training our children. My stepdaughter came to live with our family at the age of sixteen. She had recently made some poor decisions, and it was decided that it was best that she live with us for a while—though she did so reluctantly.

I tried to be the best stepmother I could be, but she resented my instruction. In turn, I took exception to her sinful behaviors in our Christian home. As a result, turmoil ensued, until one day as I prayed over the situation, God revealed He had answered one of my prayers for her. For years, I prayed for a Christian girlfriend to enter my stepdaughter's life. Duh! I suddenly realized I was to be her friend, mentor, and mother. God gave me a specific verse for my new role as a stepmother.

📖 Please read 1 Corinthians 4:2. How could this verse relate to the admonition of Proverbs 22:6?

_____

_____

_____

One of the areas in life God grants to us as a trust is our children. We are instructed to prove faithful to the best of our abilities in training them up in the way they should go. In spite of my best efforts to be a great parent, my dear stepdaughter still lives a wayward lifestyle—apart from God. On the flip side, my

"Now it is required that those who have been given a trust must prove faithful."

1 Corinthians 4:2

hyperactive son has seemingly survived my inadequate parenting skills of yesteryear to grow into a godly man. No one guarantees our efforts at parenting and mentoring will turn out as we hope. We can only do our best and then leave the results to God. But we can pray for help. So, let's close today with a prayer that we can instill godly instruction to whomever the Lord entrusts to us.

 Begin by praying these verses from Psalm 121:1–2: "*I lift up my eyes to the hills—where does my help come from? My help comes from the Lord, the Maker of heaven and earth.*"

Today's Heart-Print
Now it is required that those who have been given a trust must prove faithful.
(1 Corinthians 4:2)

Motherhood
DAY THREE

My Heart's Cry:

Father God, help me to understand that when You discipline me it is because You love and always have my best interest in mind. Teach me to discipline my children from a heart of love and not frustration, just as You do with Your children. In Jesus' name, Amen.

A Dose of Discipline

Discipline is the refining fire by which talent becomes ability—Roy L. Smith[7]

"Do you want to be on restriction, or do you want Daddy to give you a spanking? You decide."

After my two sons, ages seven and four, misbehaved by climbing on the roof of our home they were given the choice of how they were going to be disciplined. I knew my oldest son would choose a spanking. He despised being placed on restriction. However my younger son, a homebody, didn't mind being on restriction. In fact, it gave him the perfect excuse to sit around the house.

Sure enough, my oldest son received a few swats on his bottom, and the younger boy stayed home for a week. They both learned that disobedience would bring consequences. However, by allowing them some options in their punishment, I believe I averted a resentful spirit. They learned their lessons, but not at the expense of breaking their spirit.

Discipline should fit the crime and apply to the individual. As parents of children and mentors to others, we need to study what God's Word states about appropriate punishment when someone intentionally goes against authority. The topic of discipline ranges from training our children, to self-discipline, to civil authority, and church leadership. Most important is realizing that we are God's children and that He disciplines us so that we learn obedience to Him. Our Day Three section examines the Proverbs on the subject of discipline.

First, let's study God's purpose for discipline and correction. Read Hebrews 12:10–11 and then note what you discover about God and discipline.

_____

_____

_____

In our human efforts and to the best of our knowledge and ability, we discipline those we love. But God disciplines from His perfect wisdom and knowledge. When He disciplines, it produces a harvest of righteousness, even though it may be unpleasant at times. I love the statement in Hebrews 12:11, "*it* [discipline] *produces a harvest of righteousness and peace for those who have been trained by it.*" Discipline is training.

Read Proverbs 29:17 and then rewrite it in your own words.

_____

_____

_____

This proverb states, if we discipline our children in a godly manner, there is a great likelihood that they will delight us when they are adults. (Yes, they do finally mature.) I have found this true with my own children. Although at times it was difficult to be consistent in discipline, it was worth the effort. Now my adult children delight me, and I am proud to be their mother.

In contrast, what does Proverbs 29:15 state is the result of a lack of correction of a child?

_____

_____

_____

A child not corrected, may end up disgracing her parents. Obviously, there are many benefits for godly disciplining our children or poor results if discipline is neglected. Note what each of the following verses implies.

Proverbs 4:13

_____

Proverbs 6:23

_____

Proverbs 10:17

_____

Proverbs 12:1

_____

Proverbs 13:13

_____

Proverbs 13:18

_____

Discipline makes us better people. God never gives useless instruction; He always has a purpose in mind. He knows how to discipline each of us as individuals. Discipline comes in a variety of forms.

Word Study
DISCIPLINE

The term discipline found in Proverbs 29:17 is the Hebrew word is *yasar*. It means to chasten, reprove, discipline, punish, correct, instruct. It carries the connotation of either physical enforcement or verbal reinforcement. The purpose of God's discipline is changed behavior.[8] A second common word in Hebrew for discipline is *musar*, which is derived from *yasar*. *Musar* denotes the act of disciplining, punishing, and instructing. It indicates correction that results in education and often signifies oral discipline rather than corporal punishment.[9]

"Don't be afraid to correct your young ones; a spanking won't kill them."

Proverbs 23:13 (The Message)

📖 Read the following verses and match the method of correction with the correlating verse:

Proverbs 3:11   corrections

Proverbs 6:23   rebuke

Proverbs 23:13   hardships

Hebrews 12:7   spanking

📖 What does Proverbs 17:10 state?

_____

_____

Although, these proverbs clearly state that an occasional controlled spanking will not harm a child, sometimes a rebuke may be all that is necessary. Let's explore this area of discipline a little deeper.

Read Proverbs 22:15 and then consider it with Psalm 23:4b. After comparing both of these verses, how would you now define the term *"rod of discipline"*?

_____

_____

_____

I think the *"rod of discipline"* can be any tool we use to correct someone. When I looked at how the term *rod* is translated from the Hebrew word *shebet,* I learned that *shebet* can also be used to describe a "shepherd's staff."[10] Of course a shepherd uses his staff to train, guide, correct, and protect his sheep. So we might ask ourselves, what is God calling us to use as a rod of discipline when our children's actions or attitudes require correction? Instead of considering ourselves as disciplinarians, perhaps a better thought is that we are called to shepherd those whom the Lord entrusts to our care.

Today we opened with Hebrews 12:10–11. We will finish today with the same verse as our Heart-Print. Let's ask God to grant us wisdom and discernment in the area of discipline, so that a harvest of righteousness and peace will be produced.

Today's Heart-Print
"Our fathers disciplined us for a little while as they thought best; but God disciplines us for our good, that we may share in his holiness. No discipline seems pleasant at the time, but painful. Later on, however, it produces a harvest of righteousness and peace for those who have been trained by it."
(Hebrews 12:10–11)

My Lord, my Shepherd,

_____

_____

_____

_____

_____

A Legacy

The legacy we leave is not just in our possessions, but in the quality of our lives. What preparations should we be making now? The greatest waste in all of our earth, which cannot be recycled or reclaimed, is our waste of the time that God has given us each day. —Billy Graham[11]

Susanna Wesley's life changed history. How? She gave a legacy of faith to her children. Born in 1669 to a Christian minister and his wife, she grew up in a culture of devout Christian faith. Susanna imparted her understanding of Christ to her own children, instructing them in biblical knowledge and praying diligently for them an hour each day. At least once a week, she took them aside individually to discuss spiritual matters.

Her legacy to this world are John and Charles Wesley. Both of these men became leaders in the spiritual revival known as "The Great Awakening." John Wesley founded the Methodist denomination, and other Wesleyan denominations as well as theological beliefs and traditions are named after him. Charles Wesley not only preached but also wrote many of our traditional hymns.

Susanna's maternal influence bore rich fruit in these men's lives. The power of their Christian faith came about as a direct result of their godly mother. She actively lived out her faith in their home. Her accomplishments as a mother resulted in sons who continued to pass down her inheritance of faith.

Today let's examine how we can pass down a godly legacy to our children. Read Proverbs 17:6 in your Bible.

Although I am certainly not Susanna Wesley, I hope my children take pride in me as their mother. And as Proverbs 17:6 states, *"Children's children are a crown to the aged,"* I am certainly glorifying in my grandchildren. I wait with great anticipation to see what Christian heritage will pass from me, to my children, and to my adorable grandchildren.

Throughout Scripture, examples are given of women who influenced their children in a positive way. Let's look at two women whom the apostle Paul commended for their heritage in the faith.

📖 Please read 2 Timothy 1:5. List the women involved in Timothy's life.

_____

_____

What word describes their faith?

_____

📖 Timothy's grandmother Lois, and his mother Eunice, held a positive sway in the life of Timothy because of their sincere faith. According to 2 Timothy 3:14–15, what do we know for certain that Timothy learned from his grandmother and mother?

_____

_____

My Heart's Cry:

Father God, I desire to leave a legacy of faith to my children. Inspire me to pray for them daily. Instruct me on how I may leave an inheritance of godliness to my children, my grandchildren, and to others who look to me as an example. Lord, let my faith shine brightly even after I leave this earth. In Jesus' name, Amen.

"A good life gets passed on to the grandchildren."

Proverbs 13:22a (The Message)

How early in life did Timothy's religious education begin?

_____

_____

📖 Define how Proverbs 13:22a could apply to Timothy.

_____

_____

_____

Timothy certainly benefited from having a godly grandmother and mother. We know from Acts 16:1 that Timothy's mother was Jewish and a believer that Jesus was the promised Messiah. However, Timothy's father was Greek and appears not to have converted to Christianity. So evidently, Eunice and Lois modeled the Christian faith to young Timothy from infancy.

📖 Reread Proverbs 17:6 found in the margin. How would this verse apply to Lois, Timothy's grandmother?

_____

_____

Timothy and his faith certainly bring honor to Lois. Don't you think she felt proud to be his grandma? I would have! Let's look at a few Scriptures that speak about the glory of aging into a grandmother.

📖 Read Proverbs 20:29. What is the splendor of aging?

_____

_____

📖 According to Proverbs 16:31, how is this splendor attained?

_____

_____

Now granted, in our times many of us color our hair to hide the gray, but underneath the dye, it shines like a crown. A hidden crown, but still beautiful. Splendor is attained by a righteous life. Righteousness also affects our prayers for children.

Read Proverbs 15:29 and note what happens to the prayers of the righteous.

_____

_____

The Lord hears the prayers of the righteous. Praying for our children is an honor and privilege. Read the following list of prayer-points that can be lifted to the ears of God. Place a check by the ones you pray for your children. Can you think of other areas to pray for our children?

❑ safety	❑ health
❑ friends	❑ schools
❑ healing	❑ personality
❑ sports activities	❑ homework

Put Yourself in Their Shoes
TIMOTHY

Living out your faith can be difficult. Timothy actively modeled his faith in life. Read Acts 16:1–5. As an adult male, Timothy submitted to the Jewish ritual of circumcision in order to travel as a missionary with the apostle Paul. The result of his obedience? "So the churches were strengthened in the faith and grew daily in numbers" (Acts 16:5).

Truly, the list is endless. But if we want to leave an eternal legacy in this world, we need to pray for our children's walk with Jesus. Read the following verses and then note what areas of prayer are suggested.

Ephesians 1:18

_____

Ephesians 3:16

_____

Colossians 1:10

_____

2 Thessalonians 1:11

_____

Philemon 1:6

_____

Prayer changes lives. Almost every Monday, I meet with a girlfriend to pray. We pray exclusively for our children. I email each of my kids for weekly prayer requests. Plus we pray for our children to obtain Christ's glorious riches and to be encouraged in their faith. We pray they will actively share their belief in Christ with others. We ask for their hearts to have the full knowledge of the power of Jesus in their own lives.

My friend and I keep journals of prayer requests. We watch expectantly for God to answer in His divine wisdom. And then, we stand in amazement at how God works in each of their lives. I believe this effort of prayer will be a legacy for our children, not only now, but as they sift through our prayer journals after we are gone.

📖 Read Colossians 2:2 followed by Deuteronomy 29:29. What can you find that encourages you to pray for your children?

_____

_____

_____

_____

As we pray, God will reveal the mysteries of Jesus Christ to us and to our children forever. Isn't that an exciting thought?

So what will your legacy be for your children? Steve Green sings a song titled, "Find Us Faithful," written by Jon Mohr. The resounding line throughout the lyrics is "Oh may all who come behind us find us faithful." Oh Lord, let it be true for us as mentors, mothers, and grandmothers.

 It is never too late to start building a spiritual inheritance for our children. Let's begin right now. Read Today's Heart-Print. Convert this verse to a prayer in your own words. And then take a few moments to pray for your children, grandchildren and for those who you might be mentoring in their spiritual walk of faith.

Oh Father,

_____

_____

_____

_____

_____

_____

_____

_____

_____

Motherhood

DAY FIVE

My Heart's Cry:

Father, teach me to have childlike faith and obedience to You. Help me to honor my earthly parents in a manner that pleases You. Remind me of the fact, they too, are only human. I pray this in the name of Jesus, Amen.

WE THE CHILDREN

We must put away all effort to impress, and come with the guileless candor of childhood. If we do this, without a doubt God will quickly respond—
A. W. Tozer[12]

The antiseptic smell of the intensive care unit assaulted my nose as I sat next to my father's bed. Machines whirred and beeped with each labored breath he took. One collapsed lung along with the other full of pneumonia predicted the outcome for him.

"So this is how it ends," I pondered. For years, a love-hate relationship with this man influenced many of my decisions. Some good, some bad. I always sought his approval, but rarely did he grant it.

I struggled to believe my father could transform from a mean and bitter man to one full of love for others. But then one chilly October night he accepted Jesus Christ as his Savior. At the age of 79, my earthly father discovered the Father God's unconditional love. I couldn't believe it. I traveled five hundred miles just to look into those crinkled hazel eyes to see a new dad peering out at me. Our relationship changed drastically. Finally, my father became the dad I desired.

But now he lay dying. Yet strangely, I felt a deep peace. I knew he was going home to his Father in heaven. I leaned over to kiss his damp forehead and using a name I had not called him in forty-five years, I whispered, "I love you, Daddy. I'll see you soon.

We use many terms to refer to our fathers. "Father," "Poppa," "Pop," "Dad," and "Daddy" all recall certain images in our minds. Our hearts and souls were designed for a father-child type of relationship. Perhaps your experience with your father was like mine, not the best. Or maybe you had a wonderful "Daddy"; if so, count your blessings. Whatever the relationship between you and your father, remember he is human. No one is perfect. We all have faults that abound as parents and as children.

Since we have studied how to become better moms, today we will search the Scriptures to determine how we can become better children, better children not only to our earthly parents, but also to our Father in heaven.

📖 Read Ephesians 6:2–3. What does this verse say to us as children?

_____

_____

We are to honor our parents as stated in the Ten Commandments. The apostle Paul reminded the Ephesians that obedience to this commandment was linked to a special promise.

📖 Read Exodus 20:12. What is the promise related to the Fifth Commandment?

_____

_____

📖 Read Deuteronomy 5:16. What additional pledge is given in this verse?

_____

_____

God told the Israelites that if they honored their parents they would live long and it would go well with them in the Promised Land. Of course we are not the Israelites, nor are we going to a geographic location of the Promised Land. So how does this "promise" apply to us? *The Bible Background Commentary* explains it this way:

> This states a general principle that obedience fosters self-discipline, which in turn brings stability and longevity in one's life. (Stated conversely, it is improbable that an undisciplined person will live a long life. An Israelite who persistently disobeyed his parents was not privileged to enjoy a long, stable life in the land of Israel. A clear example of this was Eli's sons Hophni and Phinehas [1 Sam. 4:11].) Though that promise was given to Israel in the Old Testament, the principle still holds true today.[13]

The general concept conveys the sentiment that if someone honors their parents that person will probably live a disciplined, healthy lifestyle, which produces the tendency to live a longer life.

📖 Read Proverbs 10:27. According to this verse, what else tends to produce long life?

_____

_____

When we fear the Lord, we will obey His commandments. Obedience to His Word helps to protect us from many dangerous lifestyles and poor decisions. This principle of the Proverbs suggests that a godly, disciplined life could add health and longevity to our lives.

Extra Mile
HOPHNI AND PHINEHAS

Review the whole story of Hophni and Phinehas. Read 1 Samuel 1:3, 2:1–35, and 4:1–11. Look closely at 2:12. Besides not honoring their father, what other injustice did Eli's two sons commit? Describe the general character of the two men.

Did You Know?
CORBAN

During the time Jesus lived on earth, the traditions of the religious leaders often distorted the Word of God. The practice of giving *corban* derived from the concept of giving some type of financial gift to God. The Pharisees twisted the interpretation of Deuteronomy 23:21 to deny giving to their parents aid if it was needed. Gene Henderson explains that:

> Corban was a gift particularly designated for the Lord, and so forbidden for any other use (Mark 7:11). Jesus referred to some persons who mistakenly and deliberately avoided giving needed care to their parents by declaring as "corban" any money or goods that could otherwise be used to provide such care. Thus what began as a religious act of offering eventually functioned as a curse, denying benefit to one's own parents.[14]

Jesus chided the religious for their hypocrisy of giving gifts to God while neglecting the needs of their families. It would have been more in keeping with the Law of Moses for the leaders to have loved and honored their parents by taking financial responsibility of them if necessary, even if it meant giving less in the way of an offering to God.

📖 Now let's look at a few proverbs. Read the following verses and note what they infer.

Proverbs 23:22

_____

Proverbs 28:7

_____

Proverbs 30:11

_____

Proverbs 30:17

_____

APPLY These proverbs clearly state that we should not curse nor make fun of our parents. Nor should we disgrace them by our behavior. Can you think of a time when you intentionally embarrassed or disgraced one of your parents? What did you do? How do you feel about it now?

_____

_____

_____

I spoke harshly to and about my father many times. My bitterness and poor relationship with him produced in me a spirit of disrespect. Although we did reconcile in love, I still sinned against him for many years. I have repented of my sin of dishonoring him. Do you need to take a moment to ask God for forgiveness in this area of your life? If yes, take a moment to do so now.

📖 Read Proverbs 28:24. Place a check on the things that can be withheld from our parents.

☐ money   ☐ grandchildren
☐ possessions   ☐ time
☐ love   ☐ care giving
☐ respect   ☐ kind words

📖 Read Mark 7:6–13. What did Jesus say about the Pharisee's treatment of their parents? What did He say they nullified? (verse 13)

_____

_____

_____

The Pharisees prided themselves on following the religious laws and traditions. Yet, they manipulated the law of offerings to God in order that they would not have to give financial support to their parents. Jesus said by this action, they actually nullified the Word of God—or in essence made it of no effect.

📖 Read the following proverbs and note the emotions we may produce in our parents:

Proverbs 10:1

_____

Proverbs 15:20

_____

Proverbs 17:21

_____

Proverbs 17:25

_____

Proverbs 19:26

_____

Proverbs 23:24

_____

We have the ability to bring grief or joy, despair or rejoicing to our parents. Although, our biological parents may be gone, this principle still applies.

📖 Read the following verses and jot down their magnificent truth:

Romans 8:15–16

_____

Ephesians 5:8

_____

1 John 3:1

_____

📖 We are all children of someone. If we are Christians, we are children of God, too. What does Proverbs 20:11 state?

_____

_____

📖 A child is known by his or her actions. Read the following verses and note how others will know we are children of God.

John 13:34–35

_____

1 John 3:10

_____

1 John 3:18

_____

We are to love our parents and God with all of our actions, not just with empty words. So how did you measure up in this Day Five discourse on honoring your parents and God? Contemplate your actions. Do you honor your parents? Are there some behaviors that need to be replaced with actions and words of respect?

> "The Spirit himself testifies with our spirit that we are God's children."
>
> **Romans 8:16**

> "Even a child is known by his actions, by whether his conduct is pure and right."
>
> **Proverbs 20:11**

Take time today to consider your relationships. Ask God to give you a heart that honors Him and your parents.

Today's Heart-Print
"Dear children, let us not love with words or tongue but with actions and in truth." (1 John 3:18)

Your Heart's Impression

Journal your thoughts about . . .

the type of trust God has granted to you in regards to your children:

_____

_____

your thoughts on godly discipline in your own life:

_____

_____

What type of legacy are you leaving?

_____

_____

1. E. C. McKenzie, *14,000 Quips & Quotes For Speakers, Writers, Editors, Preachers and Teachers* (Grand Rapids, MI: Baker Book House, 1980), 380.

2. Frank S. Mead, *12,000 Religious Quotations* (Grand Rapids, MI: Baker Book House, 1989), 313.

3. Edward K. Rowell, & *Leadership Journal, 1001 Quotes, Illustrations, and Humorous Stories for Preachers, Teachers, & Writers* (Grand Rapids, MI: Baker Books, 1996), 119.

4. Spiros Zodhiates, Th.D. Exe. Ed., *Hebrew-Greek Key Study Bible, NIV Edition* (Old Testament Lexical Aids) (Chattanooga, TN: AMG Publishers, 1996), #3495, 1520.

5. Walter C. Kaiser, Jr.; Peter H. Davids; F. F. Bruce; Manfred T. Brauch, *Hard Sayings of the Bible* (Chicago, IL: InterVarsity Press, 1996), 288.

6. Zodhiates, *Hebrew-Greek Key Study Bible, NIV Edition*, 761.

7. Rowell & *Leadership Journal, 1001 Quotes, Illustrations, and Humorous Stories for Preachers, Teachers, & Writers*, 53.

8. Craig Keener, *The IVP Bible Background Commentary: New Testament.* Database © 1997, NavPress Software.

9. Zodhiates, *Hebrew-Greek Key Study Bible, NIV Edition* (Old Testament Lexical Aids), #3579, 1520.

10. Ibid., # 8657, 1555.

11. http://en.thinkexist.com/quotation/our_days_are_numbered-one_of_the_primary_goals_in/331557.html

12. Rowell & *Leadership Journal, 1001 Quotes, Illustrations, and Humorous Stories for Preachers, Teachers, & Writers*, 26.

13. Craig Keener, *The IVP Bible Background Commentary: New Testament,* in NavPress software database, 1997.

14. *Holman Bible Dictionary,* in NavPress software database, 1991.

Heart-Print of Conversation

Wise people talk because they have something to say; fools, because they have to say something.—Plato[1]

Words can make our hearts rejoice. Or words can break our hearts. Recently both rejoicing and heartbreak took place in our nation over the Sago coalmine disaster. People watched anxiously, hoping for a rescue of the miners, as minute-by-minute reports came across television screens.

I sat glued to the TV as I watched Anderson Cooper on CNN interviewing neighbors and relatives of the trapped men. Anticipation that the rescue was close at hand brought the media attention to a fevered pitch. Although, the immediate families were secluded in the Sago Baptist Church awaiting notification of their loved ones, the reporters still pressed on for more information.

Suddenly, a joyous shout rose up from somewhere nearby the church. Newscasters declared and print media sported these words, "We've got twelve alive!" as well as "Believe in Miracles: Twelve Miners Found Alive."

I whispered a prayer of thanksgiving. Tired from the long day, I yawned and went to bed with a sense of relief.

Until the next morning when I clicked on the news, the headlines now read, "Eleven Dead, One Alive."

What?

Words can make our hearts rejoice; they can also break our hearts.

Miscommunication of words brought the ecstasy of joy to feelings of anger, resentment, and despair. The mine command center had misheard what the rescue team relayed from below ground. Soon the miscommunication spread to family members gathered inside the church, and then to the crowd outside, to the competitive media, and to me sitting in my living room 2,500 miles away.

This tragedy displayed the power of words. Our conversations hold more power than anything else we possess. This week we will study how to wield them with skill and wisdom.

WINDY WORDS

It takes two years to learn to talk and seventy years to learn to control your mouth.
—Unknown

Kids say funny things. Several television shows, books, emails, and jokes all derive from hilarious statements spouted from the mouths of children. Sometimes they speak truth, when they should keep quiet. Other times, they turn words around in such a way that it mortifies their parents.

When my son was little, he enjoyed watching *The Muppets*. He especially liked Kermit and Miss Piggy. However, a problem arose because his babysitter's name was Peggy. Peggy's hefty size somehow translated to my toddler's mindset as Miss Piggy. He would call her Miss Piggy and no amount of my trying to correct the "Piggy" to "Peggy" worked. Needless to say, as his redfaced mother I was at a loss for words.

I think our Father, certainly must shake His head at our words. We use our mouths so carelessly. He wants us to speak in a way that points others to Him, not away. God even gives us a textbook, the Bible, which is full of instruction on how to handle our wayward tongues. Today let's look at what He teaches us in Proverbs.

📖 Read Proverbs 23:15–16.

What do these words tell you about what we say and how God might feel about our words?

_____

_____

_____

Don't you just love the phrase, *my inmost being will rejoice when your lips speak what is right*? I want God to rejoice when I speak. In addition, I want to bless others when I open my mouth. Let's look at a few different proverbs about today's topic of conversation.

📖 Please read the following proverbs and note their admonitions for our conversations.

My Heart's Cry:

Lord, throughout this week teach me how to use my words wisely and with gentleness. Reveal to me how my words can bless or hurt others. I ask that You make me more aware of every word I say. In Your name, Amen.

Proverbs 4:24

_____

Proverbs 10:11

_____

Proverbs 16:23

_____

Proverbs 21:23

_____

Proverbs 25:11

_____

We need to rid ourselves of any type of perverse speech. In the next few days, we will discover all types of conversations that God considers out of line for a godly woman. We want hearts of wisdom to guide and guard spoken exchanges, so that our mouths become like righteous fountains that give verbal gifts.

📖 Now let's note specifically what is beneficial to our verbal communication.

Proverbs 17:4

_____

Proverbs 17:20

_____

Proverbs 18:13

_____

Proverbs 27:14

_____

We have studied about wisdom and folly in previous lessons, but today let's look at what the Bible tells us about a wise or foolish tongue. Circle the portion that describes a wise use of the tongue and underline what God considers as foolish.

Proverbs 13:3
"He who guards his lips guards his life, but he who speaks rashly will come to ruin."

Proverbs 15:2
"The tongue of the wise commends knowledge, but the mouth of the fool gushes folly."

Proverbs 15:7
"The lips of the wise spread knowledge; not so the hearts of fools."

Word Study
INMOST BEING

The Hebrew words translated "inmost being" in Proverbs 23:16 encompass the thought of the kernel of our innermost self, the heart, the mind, and the spirit.

PROVERBS 10:31–32

"The mouths of the righteous (those harmonious with God) bring forth skillful and godly Wisdom, but the perverse tongue shall be cut down [like a barren and rotten tree] The lips of the [uncompromisingly] righteous know [and therefore utter] what is acceptable, but the mouth of the wicked knows [and therefore speaks only] what is obstinately willful and contrary." (The Amplified Bible)

SEVERED TONGUES

Does it sound harsh to cut out someone's perverse tongue? Although, not specifically mentioned in Mosaic law, it could have been rendered acceptable under Exodus 21:24–25, *"eye for eye, tooth for tooth, hand for hand, foot for foot, burn for burn, wound for wound, bruise for bruise."* Although probably not common in the Hebrew culture, surrounding cultures practiced severing the tongue for punishment or torture.

Proverbs 19:1
"Better a poor man whose walk is blameless than a fool whose lips are perverse."

📖 Now please read Proverbs 10:31–32 in the margin. Why does this verse correlate with our first verse in today's lesson? (Proverbs 23:15–16?)

_____

_____

_____

Now reread Proverbs 10:31–32 and compare it to what Jesus said in Matthew 15:17–20. Where do the things we say actually come from?

_____

_____

Our words come from the attitudes of our hearts. Think back to the toddlers you know that have said funny things. Regardless of their hard-to-understand baby talk, they usually all have one word in common. It's one of the first words they learn to say: "No!" Right from early childhood our nature is to be obstinate and contrary to God's will. Our words come from our hearts. If we want to make our heavenly Father rejoice, then we must decide to clean-up our hearts and our mouths.

Today's Heart-Print
My son, if your heart is wise, then my heart will be glad; my inmost being will rejoice when your lips speak what is right. (Proverbs 23:15–16)

Father,

_____

_____

_____

_____

_____

_____

_____

_____

_____

Conversation

DAY TWO

OUT WITH THE TRASH

A slip of the foot you may soon recover, but a slip of the tongue you may never get over—Benjamin Franklin[2]

Today's paper read, "Nearly three-quarters of Americans questioned last week—seventy-four percent—said they encounter profanity in public frequently or occasionally, according to an Associated Press poll. Two-thirds said they think people swear more than they did twenty years ago."[3]

As a teenage girl, I could swear like a sailor. And if you caught me in an irritable mood, I might have cursed you to your face. Gratefully, soon after I became a believer, my bad language was one of the first "bad habits" to depart from my life. However, I still surprise myself with an occasional "oops" type of word.

Cursing and profanity run rampant in our culture. We hardly notice any more when we hear profanity on the radio, the television, or in the movies. Howard Stern would excuse it as free speech, but that's not what God calls it.

The Bible has a lot to say about our foolish tongues and the junk that streams forth. In Day Two, we'll study trash talk and how to get rid of it.

📖 Read Proverbs 10:19.

How would you explain the meaning of this proverb to a young child?

_____

_____

 I think I would say something like "The more we talk, the more trouble we can get ourselves into." I know from experience that the more I keep my mouth shut, the less I need to ask forgiveness from others. Do you agree? Let's brainstorm some ways we might sin with our mouths. Jot down as many as you can think of.

_____

_____

_____

_____

📖 OK, now let's look at Scripture and see if we came up with similar things. Match the following verses with the correct passages.

Proverbs 6:16, 17, 19	false witness
Proverbs 10:18	lies
Proverbs 19:5	curse
Proverbs 30:11	slander

📖 Certainly, there are many ways to misuse our mouths. Let's review one of the Ten Commandments. Please read Exodus 20:7 in the side margin.

In what ways do we misuse the name of the Lord?

_____

_____

 Using any form of God's name with empty or frivolous meaning is considered misuse. Take a few moments to consider if you carelessly misuse the name of God. If yes, make a note of when, where, and why.

_____

_____

_____

My Heart's Cry:

Father, I ask Your Holy Spirit to enable me to learn to control my mouth. I want to be a good witness for You. Amen.

"You shall not misuse the name of the Lord your God, for the Lord will not hold anyone guiltless who misuses his name."

Exodus 20:7

📖 Now let's look at another way Scripture tells us that we might use our tongue in a negative manner. After reading each verse, what did you discover about their similarities?

Proverbs 10:8

_____

Proverbs 10:10

_____

1 Timothy 6:20

_____

2 Timothy 2:16

_____

What in your life do you consider godless chatter?

_____

_____

_____

When I jabber away about something inconsequential, I think to myself, _Just stop talking; it doesn't matter_. Do you ever think like that? If yes, list five topics that often turn into godless chatter.

1. _____
2. _____
3. _____
4. _____
5. _____

First on my list was politics and then religion. People often debate these two issues when the only purpose is to win the argument. I remember reading a quote that described this type of godless chatter. "A person convinced against his will, is of the same opinion still." I can relate! Since I am not a good debater, I lose the argument but leave the discussion with exactly the same opinion I started the conversation with.

APPLY What about dirty jokes, off-color remarks, racial remarks? Or the "water-cooler" discussions at work?

Can you give an example of how any of these areas has applied to you?

_____

_____

How do you think godless chatter affects non-believers who hear us prattle away?

_____

_____

When we make prejudicial statements against people, non-believers do not see us as a loving people, but instead they see us as judgmental. They perceive us to be hypocrites. When we participate in "dirty jokes" or waste our work time with useless talk, we tarnish our witness for Jesus Christ.

📖 Finally, let's look at another way God considers our words to be useless. Read Matthew 6:5–12. What does Jesus say in verse 7?

_____

_____

📖 It shocks us to think that our prayers might sound like babbling to God, doesn't it? Reread verses 9–12. In this familiar prayer, the Lord's Prayer, did you see how direct and non-repetitive Jesus' model prayer is?

■ The Lord's Prayer is direct and conversational. It doesn't repeat a word or phrase over and over again. It is a model of how we should pray.

■ It acknowledges God the Father for His holiness and authority.

■ It requests provision for daily needs

■ It teaches us to ask forgiveness for our sins

■ It teaches us to ask for help to live holy and godly lives.

■ God doesn't want us to babble to others or to Him. He wants us to pray with our minds engaged and actively seeking intimate communion with Him.

📖 Read Proverbs 13:2–3. Looking at the over-all context, how would these verses apply to today's study?

_____

_____

Our lips speak words that can produce enjoyment or have the ability to bring us to ruin. We must learn to guard our tongue in such areas as profanity, cursing, slander, and godless chatter.

Today as we close, write a prayer to the Father that models the Lord's Prayer, but with your own words and specific needs. Ask Him to help you guard your tongue so that you may honor Him.

_____

_____

_____

_____

_____

_____

_____

_____

Today's Heart-Print
"When words are many, sin is not absent, but he who holds his tongue is wise."
(Proverbs 10:19)

LIAR MOUTH

"No man has a good enough memory to make a successful liar."
—Abraham Lincoln[4]

My Heart's Cry:

Oh Lord, give me the courage to speak the truth. When the thought of a "fib" floats through my thoughts, remind me that You are Truth and You desire for me to speak truth. Lord, I thank You that You always speak the truth to me in love; help me to do likewise with others.

More than twenty years ago, a *Time Magazine* reporter discovered some peculiar facts about Jack Nicholson's family heritage.

The reporter questioned Mr. Nicholson on why he had lied about his mother. Nicholson had told him his mother was Ethel May Nicholson. However the reporter discovered that June, who supposedly was Nicholson's sister, was the biological mother. Ethel May was in reality his grandmother.

Why had Nicholson lied to him? He hadn't. This was the first time Nicholson had learned of the cover-up himself. At the time of his birth, the stigma of an unwed woman giving birth was so great that the whole family had conspired to keep the truth a secret. "Such is the price of fame," he later quipped. "People start poking around in your private life, and the next thing you know your sister is actually your mother."[5]

Now this may sound strange, but you would be surprised to find out just how many people discover siblings as parents and who knows what else when the truth comes out. Several years ago, I found out that my mother and father gave a child up for adoption just eleven months prior to my birth. I was always told, "You're so lucky you are an only child." Later I discovered I also had a half-sister. Wow! Truth may shock and hurt, but it usually sneaks out of its dank hiding place of deceit.

Today we will study the sin of a lying tongue. The Proverbs have much to say when it comes to conversational honesty.

📖 Read Proverbs 12:22 and then fill-in the blanks.

"The Lord _____ lying lips, but he _____ in men who are _____."

📖 The Lord detests lying lips, but He delights in us when we are truthful. The problem is lies come so easily to us. Please read Genesis 18:9–15.

What did Sarah lie about?

_____

Why did she lie?

_____

_____

What did the Lord say to her?

_____

_____

How do you think Sarah felt afterward?

_____

_____

It seems like such a little fib doesn't it? White lies, little untruths, pop from our mouths from an early age. I am certain she felt guilty and awkward when confronted about her lie. Let's review some of our own incidents of lying.

Can you remember the first time you told a lie? If yes, what was it?

_____

_____

In high school what type of lies did you most typically tell?

_____

_____

In what situations are you now most prone to lie or stretch the truth?

_____

_____

_____

The first lie I recall telling was when I was about three or four. I told my mother a lie about my dad. I still remember how hurt and angry he became with me. Later in high school, I skipped many classes which gave me ample opportunities to lie when asked about my day at school.

Now, I find myself apt to lie when I think I might hurt someone's feelings. You know the questions that we get asked like, "Do I look fat?" It seems far nicer to lie than to speak the brutal truth to a friend.

One of my pastors uses this example to help demonstrate the ability to speak the truth, yet not offend. When a young mom asked, "Isn't my baby cute?", if she wasn't a darling tot, he would reply, "Well, now *that's* a baby!" I need to learn to be more creative in my truthful responses. How about you? Let's move on to see what else we can learn about speaking the truth.

📖 Read the following two proverbs. What do you discover about the longevity of lies?

Proverbs 12:19

_____

Proverbs 21:6

_____

In the movie *Liar, Liar* the character portrayed by Jim Carrey, Fletcher Reede, lies to everyone, ranging from his young son, ex-wife, clients, on down to his co-workers. For a birthday wish, Fletcher's son wishes that his father would not tell a single lie for twenty-four hours straight. In an "only-in-Hollywood" scenario, the boy's wish is supernaturally granted somehow, and Fletcher soon discovers that his biggest "asset" (his knack at being a liar mouth) has suddenly become his biggest liability. Not only is Fletcher unable to tell a lie; he cannot keep himself from telling people exactly what he's thinking, even when such honesty is painful to others or embarrassing to him. We laugh at the predicaments Fletcher gets himself into, but in reality, lying is harmful to others and to ourselves.

Did You Know?
WHAT TANGLED WEB WE WEAVE

When we attempt to deceive someone with our words, our bodies undergo certain physiological responses when we attempt to deceive someone. That's how polygraph machines (lie detectors) identify that a person is lying. When a person lies, the machine picks up changes in heart rate, respiratory rate, and blood pressure. It also tracks how much our fingertips sweat when we lie!

> *"God can't stomach liars; he loves the company of those who keep their word."*
>
> ## Proverbs 12:22 (The Message)

📖 In the following proverbs, what do you discover about the end result of lies?

Proverbs 19:9

_____

Proverbs 26:28

_____

People who lie hurt others, and these actions will not go unpunished. The punishment may be seen or unseen, but God knows the truth. He will justly discipline those who lie.

📖 According to Proverbs 19:22, it is better to be poor than to be a liar. Why do you think this statement is true?

_____

_____

The absence of truth in someone's life points to a lack of character. From God's viewpoint, it is more beneficial to live in poverty than to possess a corruptness that illustrates itself by lying.

📖 According to John 14:6 who is Truth?

Jesus says, He is *"the Way, the Truth, and the Life"* As followers and companions of Jesus, we must speak truth. The apostle Paul succinctly sums up this concept in Colossians 3:9–10. Please copy this verse and consider its significance to you.

_____

_____

_____

> *"Two things I ask of you, O Lord; do not refuse me before I die: Keep falsehood and lies far from me; give me neither poverty nor riches, but give me only my daily bread."*
>
> ## Proverbs 30:7–8

🙏 Since we have put off our old self when we accepted Christ as Lord of our lives, we should not continue to lie. We should imitate Jesus, our Truth. Read Proverbs 30:7–8 in the margin and then make it your prayer to God today.

Today's Heart-Print
"The Lord detests lying lips, but he delights in men who are truthful"
(Proverbs 12:22).

Lord Jesus,

_____

_____

_____

_____

_____

_____

_____

_____

GALLOPING GOSSIP

Conversation is an exercise of the mind, but gossiping is an exercise of the tongue—Unknown[6]

Do you remember when you were little and you played the game "Gossip"? Everyone would sit in a big circle and someone would whisper a long sentence, just once, in the next person's ear. As the phrase went from one person to another its distortion became so great that by the time it was repeated to the person who started the game, it was usually unrecognizable as the same expression.

We still play into the game of gossip. We read all sorts of slanderous words about celebrities. Often we don't know with certainty that any of these words are true. Most evening "entertainment" television shows tattle about another superstar's marriage breakup and speculate on the intimate details of why, how, and when. It is gossip; we listen, and we love it.

However, God doesn't think highly of gossip, whether we are the instigators of hearsay or just listeners. Today's let's look at His opinion of gossip.

📖 Please read Proverbs 11:13. What two things do we learn from this proverb?

_____

_____

_____

APPLY A trustworthy person can keep a secret, but a gossip betrays others. I think we can all relate to this proverb on one level or another. Will you note examples that you have experienced for each of the following?

A time you felt betrayed by the words of someone.

_____

_____

When have you gossiped about someone?

_____

_____

Describe someone who keeps your secrets.

_____

_____

Do you consider yourself able to keep someone else's secrets?

_____

_____

I know the feeling of being betrayed by someone spreading gossip about me. It hurts! But I am guilty of talking about other people too. Usually in the

My Heart's Cry:

Dear Lord, Please grant me the courage to walk away from hearsay when it begins. I ask for wisdom in my own conversations. Give me a nudge when gossipy thoughts enter my mind, and stop them from flowing through my tongue. Amen.

Did You Know?
GOSSIP

Although we relate to the word, "gossip" with a negative connation, the original meaning of "gossip" held a positive meaning. It referred to a godparent or blood relative. Over time "gossip" developed into a term that reflected destructive and damaging conversation, usually in reference to women speaking to one another about someone else. Still today, the stereotypes that formed centuries ago are prevalent in society. Men are rarely referred to as gossips, or their conversations deemed gossip. "Gossip" is considered to be a negative aspect conversation engaged in by women.[8]

context of the word "gossip," it refers to women. Do you think women gossip more than men do? Explain your answer.

_____

_____

_____

📖 When we read Scriptures that concern the topic of gossip, they unfortunately seem to point the finger of gossip primarily to women. Read 1 Timothy 5:11–13 and note what verse 13 states regarding women and the potential dangers of loose conversation.

_____

_____

This verse warns us of a woman's propensity toward gossip and becoming a busybody. Rate on the following scale, the amount of gossip you may say or listen to in a week's time.

⬅———————————————————————➡

Never   Once a week   Three to four times a week   Everyday

I wish I could say I never participate in gossip. However, many times I am deep in a conversation before I realize it has turned into a full-fledged gossip session.

📖 Let's look at a few more proverbs and what they say about gossip. Read the following proverbs and note what you learn from each one.

Proverbs 16:28

_____

Proverbs 17:9

_____

Proverbs 20:19

_____

Gossip separates close friends. People who talk too much usually end up betraying a confidence. People get hurt or worse. There was an old World War II slogan that stated, "Loose lips sink ships." This meant that if someone betrayed a confidence or spread rumors about what or where our soldiers were headed, those loose lips could potentially result in American troops losing a battle or even their lives.

📖 Now please read the following two proverbs.

Proverbs 18:8
Proverbs 26:22

What unusual thing did you discover?

_____

_____

_____

"Silence is often misinterpreted, but never misquoted."

—Unknown

Why do you think God would repeat these words?

_____

_____

What do these words mean to you?

_____

_____

_____

Did you find it unusual that these verses are identical? When the Bible repeats something, there is a good chance that God has placed special emphasis on the repeated information for our benefit. Here, God wants us to know that gossip might seem tantalizing or rewarding at the moment, but when we tell rumors or listen to tales, they go down to rest in our heart. It's hard to refuse a delicious dessert, and it seems equally difficult not to listen to a bit of juicy gossip. But taking just one crumb of either one creates a craving for more. Hearing and speaking gossip is just like consuming our favorite food; once ingested, it assimilates into our innermost being and is retained and remembered with fondness. It becomes habit forming. Unlike food consumption, feeding off gossip will not sustain us. Though the verses do not spell this out, it is implied in Proverbs 18 and 26 that gossiping is enjoyable for a season but, like many of the foods we eat, doesn't digest well. There will be unintended consequences for the unguarded words we speak.

📖 Let's take a look at how God compares gossip to other sins. List what other sins are clumped together with gossip.

Romans 1:29–30

_____

2 Corinthians 12:20

_____

Although we know that gossip contributes to quarreling, jealousy, and outbursts of anger, did you think that gossip would rank along side the sins of greed, evil, murder, and malice? The Bible categorizes gossip and slander in a list of what we often refer to as the "seven deadly sins." While we are studying gossip, let's take a peek at its twin sister *slander.*

What does Proverbs 10:18b reveal to us about slander?

_____

_____

When we slander others, we behave as fools. Why? Slander harms people. It includes the secret whispering of lies about others, but slander also occurs when we spread unfortunate truths about people behind their backs. In our society, the act of slandering another can be prosecuted in court. In newspapers, we read about slander cases where huge amounts of monetary reimbursement are awarded to the slander victims. To slander anyone is a foolish thing to do.

📖 Please read Proverbs 30:10.

 Can you think of a situation where the truth of this proverb has manifested itself in the work place?

 Word Study
SLANDER

Proverbs 10:18 refers to the term slander that comes from the Hebrew word, *dibbah*. It derives from a feminine noun meaning slander or a bad report. It describes a report of for an evil purpose to defame someone. Proverbs warns that not only can it destroy the person defamed, but also the person who spreads the story.

_____

_____

Whether evidenced in a corporate work environment, in a layperson's ministry, or in a volunteer working for a civic organization, slander destroys. If you slander someone, remember that the tables could be turned, and you could end up being the one hurt.

📖 After reading Proverbs 26:20, what would remedy the sins of gossip and slander?

_____

_____

_____

We must refuse to listen to slander. We must train ourselves not to ignite or continue to inflame gossip. Gossip is like a fire. Without oxygen a fire goes out, without listening ears or slanderous tongues, gossip will extinguish itself in our lives.

Let's close today's lesson with some moments of *mouth reflection*. Describe to God how you plan to avoid gossip and slander in the future. Ask Him for guidance in this area.

_____

_____

_____

_____

Today's Heart-Print
"The words of a gossip are like choice morsels; they go down to a man's inmost parts." (Proverbs 18:8)

Dear God,

_____

_____

_____

_____

_____

_____

_____

_____

_____

_____

_____

MODELING GODLY GIRL TALK

The great test of a man's character is his tongue—Oswald Chambers[7]

We sat on the sofa chatting. Girlfriend to girlfriend, we laughed and shared secrets. We giggled over the private details of our lives.

Meanwhile, my friend's young daughter played under her "tent." The tent's tarp, a soft yellow blanket draped over an armchair and the coffee table. She played, we talked. Every so often, we could hear her talking softly to her dolls. Occasionally, her tennis shoe would whack one of our ankles as it jerked out of her homemade playhouse.

Although we assumed we were as imperceptible to her as she was invisible to us, we were not. Suddenly we heard her delicate little voice, "instructing" her dolls about how to deal with a mean friend. And then, we heard her repeat a discussion that should have been for adult ears only.

We looked at each other ashamed. Instead of modeling godly girl talk, we had exposed a young child to mean-hearted gossip. Her tender little ears heard a conversation of words that she should not have been exposed to until she was much older. We should have known better.

So today, we are going to look at how we can use conversation to bless and encourage others by modeling godly girl talk. Let's get started.

📖 What theme can you discover from the following proverbs?

Proverbs 10:13–14

_____

Proverbs 14:3

_____

Proverbs 16:23

_____

I think Proverbs 16:23 sums up all the others we have looked at in this lesson: *"A wise man's heart guides his mouth, and his lips promote instruction."* When we use wisdom in our speech, we won't be fools, but our lips will model godly conversation.

📖 Please match the following proverb with its matching phrase.

Proverbs 10:20   Lips of the righteous know what is fitting.
Proverbs 10:21   Tongue of the righteous is choice silver.
Proverbs 10:32   Lips of the righteous nourish many.

Do you see how righteous words help others? Righteous lips know what is fitting to say and are like pure silver. These thoughts tie in with another proverb. Please read Proverbs 12:14 in the margin. How does this proverb correlate with the above proverbs?

My Heart's Cry:

Father, I want to model to other women godly girl talk. Teach me to use words of encouragement, so that others may be blessed. Help me to set an example for girls who are young and just learning how to converse. Lord, above all, I want to please You in how I speak. In Jesus' name, Amen.

"From the fruit of his lips a man is filled with good things as surely as the work of his hands rewards him."

Extra Mile
JAMES 3

The Book of James has a lot to say about how we use our tongues. Read James Chapter 3. Then go back through this lesson and journal how James 3 applies to the five different topics we examined, which include words that glorify God, trash talk, lying, gossip, and being a good example in our conversations.

Now would you apply Proverbs 12:14 with the fruit of the Spirit found in Galatians 5:22?

In past lessons, we have studied that attitudes residing inside of us usually spill forth from our mouths. When we are filled with good things, love, joy, peace, gentleness, and kindness, our lips will share these attributes as well. When we are righteous inside, it will be evident on the outside in our lips being used to bless others.

📖 Please read the following proverbs and then write examples applicable to yourself and to others.

Proverbs 9:9

Proverbs 15:1

Proverbs 15:4

Proverbs 16:21

What instruction does Proverbs 31:8–9 gives us?

We need to speak up when we see injustice. Can you give an example of a time when you witnessed an injustice yet remained silent? Or perhaps, you spoke up, resulting in a positive change for the situation? Explain how you felt in either case.

_____

_____

What benefits do we find when we use our tongues for encouragement?

Proverbs 15:23

_____

_____

Proverbs 16:24

_____

_____

When our hearts are wise, then we will use wisdom when we speak. But engaging in foolish talk, as my friend and I did, can bring damage. Let's bring this lesson to a close with one final verse from the New Testament. Read James 1:26. Prayerfully, consider this verse and write a prayer asking God to help you to keep a tight rein on your tongue.

Today's Heart-Print
"A wise man's heart guides his mouth, and his lips promote instruction."
(Proverbs 16:23)

Father God,

_____

_____

_____

_____

_____

Your Heart's Impression
Journal your thoughts about how powerful words can be in your life.

_____

_____

_____

Describe and contemplate an area where you struggle the most: lying, gossiping, or just misusing God's name.

_____

_____

_____

_____

How do you influence others with your conversations?

_____

_____

_____

How can you begin to model godly girl talk?

_____

_____

_____

_____

Tell the Lord God what is in your heart after this week's lesson.

_____

_____

_____

_____

_____

_____

_____

_____

_____

_____

_____

_____

1. http://www.worldofquotes.com/author/Plato/1/index.html

2. http://www.quotationspage.com/quotes/Benjamin_Franklin/

3. http://www.msnbc.msn.com/id/12063093/

4. E. C. McKenzie, *14,000 Quips & Quotes For Speakers, Writers, Editors, Preachers and Teacher,* (Grand Rapids, MI: Baker Book House, 1980), 300.

5. http://www.jacknicholson.org/Time.html

6. McKenzie, *14,000 Quips & Quotes*, 213.

7. Max Anders, *Holman Old Testament Commentary-Proverbs* (Nashville, TN: Holman Reference, 2005), 206.

8. http://kpearson.faculty.tcnj.edu/Dictionary/gossip.htm

9. Warren Baker, D.R.E. and Eugene Carpenter, Ph.D., eds., *The Complete Word Study Dictionary Old Testament* (Chattanooga, TN: AMG Publishers, 2003). #

Heart-Print of Finances

Stewardship is what a man does after he says, "I believe"—W.H. Greever[1]

Many people, especially women, enjoy vacationing on luxury cruise ships. There's nothing quite like enjoying the sights and sounds of the high seas while living in the lap of luxury. For starters, there's the luxury of having everything you need magically appear in your room, on deck, or while dining. Then there's the luxury of having cabin stewards make sure your bed is turned down at night, and—better yet—made in the morning! And then what about room service bringing fresh laundered towels each day while they scoop up the ones left in a heap on the floor?

Poolside stewards provide iced tea, water, or whatever your thirst craves with just a flick of your hand toward the lounge chair. Table servers during the dinner hour help with your napkin, serve luscious creative meals, and refill your coffee unobtrusively. And then someone, somewhere within the large ship does the dishes.

That's the reason we like to vacation on ocean liners. We like the fact that stewards make provisions for our every need. Their jobs are to manage our vacation so that we arrive home with positive stories to tell other potential sailors about the restful trip we took.

In God's economy, stewardship is given to us. He allows us to take care of His property. He wants us to use our resources wisely and in godly ways. In this lesson, we will explore the topic of finances. So what do you think? Is God happy with our stewardship?

> **In God's economy, He allows us to take care of His property.**

WHAT'S IN YOUR WALLET?

Make all you can, save all you can, give all you can—John Wesley[2]

My Heart's Cry:

Dear God, I admit I like to have control over my money. This lesson points me to the areas where I could be a better steward of not only my money, but of any material blessing that You have given me. Amen.

We are a nation of over-consumers. We buy more than our homes can hold, so we rent storage units to hold our useless stuff. We spend hundreds of dollars on the newest diet craze, because we overeat. We need a vacation after our vacation since we wore ourselves out on leisure travel.

Consider these statistics. It makes me ponder what God thinks of us.

- 75 percent of the world's population may not have food, shelter, or clothing.
- More than 700 million people have experienced starvation, war, or religious oppression.
- Only 5 percent of the world's population saves money, purchases wants instead of needs and still has money to throw into a change basket.[3]

 I know I belong to that five percent of the world's wealthy. What about you? Answer the following questions to see how much wealth you have in comparison to the world.

How many televisions are in your home?

How many cars do you own?

How many meals and snacks do you consume each day?

Do you own a computer?

These questions are not designed to make us feel guilty, but to help keep our finances in perspective. God gives us money and possessions as a gift and a blessing.

📖 Read Proverbs 10:22 and Ecclesiastes 5:19. Journal your thoughts below.

_____

_____

_____

_____

_____

We should not feel guilt over our blessings. In Day One we will delve into how to be good stewards of God's generous gifts. We could easily sum up this entire lesson's teaching by quoting 1 Timothy 6:10.

According to this verse what is the root of all kind of evils?

_____

It is the *love* of money, not money itself. What reason does this verse give for living life free from the love of money?

_____

When we love money and pursue wealth, we are in danger of wandering away from the faith, which can produce many griefs. God wants us to trust Him with our needs. If He decides to grant us wealth, there will be no trouble attached with it.

How does Hebrews 13:5 compare to 1 Timothy 6:10?

_____

_____

_____

Both verses speak of the love of money. First Timothy 6:10 carries a warning and Hebrews 13:5 promises that God will never leave us nor forsake us. These verses encourage us to be content with the material gain God provides instead of craving it in an unwholesome way.

What happens when we are not content with our money? Ecclesiastes 5:10 reveals the answer. Please fill in the blanks.

"Whoever loves _____ never has money _____; whoever loves wealth is never _____ with his income. This too is _____."

Most people discover that the more money you have, the more you seem to want. I recall watching a biographical special on TV about a popular country western singer. At the time, he stated, "I have more money than my children, my grandchildren, or my great-grandchildren could ever spend." Yet today, this same musical artist hawks his old CD's as if he needs milk for his children. When is enough, enough?

📖 Jot down what the following three verses have in common.

1 Timothy 3:3

_____

2 Timothy 3:2

_____

1 Peter 5:2

_____

Please remember our truth learned from the previous lesson that when the Word of God restates a principle or concept repeatedly it screams, "Pay attention! This is important!" These verses reiterate the principle for us to be free of the love of money and greed. So how important is our heart attitude toward being greedy for money from God's perspective?

Obviously, it is very important. So let's see what Proverbs has to say about money and greed. In the following proverbs, match the verse with the description of greed.

Proverbs 11:26	Greed brings trouble to your family.
Proverbs 15:27a	It's better to have a little, than gain a lot with injustice.
Proverbs 16:8	People curse those who hoard.

Let's take a close look at a few verses to find out what we as believers *should* do first with the blessings of our income. Write down the instructions given in each verse.

> *"For the love of money is a root of all kinds of evil. Some people, eager for money, have wandered from the faith and pierced themselves with many griefs."*
>
> *1 Timothy 6:10*

Proverbs 3:9

_____

Deuteronomy 26:1–3; 12

_____

Now we are going to head in a slightly different direction. Read Deuteronomy 6:16 and Matthew 4:7. What are we told not to do?

_____

_____

_____

In both these verses, we are told not to test the Lord God. However, what does Malachi 3:10 state about testing God on the area of our giving and our finances?

_____

_____

This verse is the only verse in the Bible that God says, "Test me." Although, this verse was given in the Old Testament, the concept still applies to New Testament believers in that we should give freely to God, anticipating that He will supply our needs—maybe not our wants, but our needs. This is how the _Bible Knowledge Commentary_ explains it,

> One must be careful in applying these promises to believers today. The Mosaic Covenant, with its promises of material blessings to Israel for her obedience, is no longer in force. However, the New Testament speaks about generosity and giving. While not requiring a tithe of believers today, the New Testament does speak of God's blessing on those who give generously to the needs of the church and especially to those who labor in the Word.[4]

Throughout the Bible, we are encouraged to give generously. Read the following verses and match their instruction.

Matthew 17:24–26	give to the poor
Proverbs 28:27	give cheerfully
2 Corinthians 9:7	give generously
2 Corinthians 9:11	pay our taxes

Let's look at one more bit of instruction found in 1 Corinthians 16:2. Please fill in the blanks to help cement this principle in your thoughts.

_On the first day of every week, each one of you should set aside a sum of _____ in keeping with his _____, saving it up, so that when I come no collections will have to be made._ (1 Corinthians 16:2)

As children of God, we are to give generously and cheerfully. We need to pay our taxes honestly. We must give to the poor. In Day Two, we will take a closer look at our obligation and privilege of giving to the poor. But as we conclude today's lesson, please read Today's Heart-Print and then rewrite what it means to you.

" 'Bring the whole tithe into the storehouse, that there may be food in my house. Test me in this,' says the Lord Almighty, 'and see if I will not throw open the floodgates of heaven and pour out so much blessing that you will not have room enough for it.' "

Malachi 3:10

"Do not wear yourself out to get rich; have the wisdom to show restraint. Cast but a glance at riches, and they are gone, for they will surely sprout wings and fly off to the sky like an eagle." (Proverbs 23:4–5)

Offer a prayer of thanksgiving to our God for the bounty and blessings in your life.

Oh gracious Father,

_____

_____

_____

_____

_____

_____

_____

_____

_____

GIVE IT AWAY!

We make a living by what we get; we make a life by what we give
—Winston Churchill[5]

A barefoot homeless man trekked through our neighborhood. His dirty, matted hair looked like it hadn't been shampooed in months. His tattered clothes hung from his thin frame. However, his feet haunted my mind. Barefoot he trudged up and down our hilly street. His soles appeared swollen with bruises. I could distinguish the thick calluses and cracks of his unprotected feet.

The weather started to turn chilly, and still each evening he wandered up the hill, to where he slept in some protected cleft of the nearby mountain. As Christmas approached, I wrapped a few gifts for him. Some socks, clog style shoes, a large fleece blanket and various fast food gift cards.

As I drove home late one afternoon, I saw him. I raced home, and I sent my nineteen-year-old son to present the gifts to the destitute man.

To our amazement, he rejected the offering. He told my son, "Tell your mother that I will not take it. I will not accept gifts that are only given because of the 'season of the year.'"

I then thought to myself, *Hmmm. . . . I guess I need to represent Jesus all year round, in my gift giving.*

As I study Scripture, I realize I need to give generously to the poor. All the time. Most of us are very familiar with this principle. However, I believe we need to review it on a regular basis and put it into practice.

My Heart's Cry:

Father, give me a generous heart. Allow my eyes to see the vision of what can be accomplished when I use my money for eternal purposes. In Jesus' name, Amen.

> ## "Rich and poor have this in common: The Lord is the Maker of them all."
>
> ### Proverbs 22:2

📖 Read Proverbs 22:2 in the margin. What do the poor and wealthy have in common?

_____

_____

APPLY The Lord is maker of the poor and wealthy. Let's read the familiar parable of the Good Samaritan. Then answer the following questions, but let your answers be reflective of today's society.

📖 Read Luke 10:25–37.

Where would Samaria be in your town?

_____

Who might be a "Levite"?

_____

How many Christians do you think would pass by?

_____

Who would be someone you might think of as an unexpected "Good Samaritan?"

_____

_____

More importantly what would you do?

_____

_____

What does Proverbs 19:17 tell us?

_____

_____

> ## "He who is kind to the poor lends to the Lord, and he will reward him for what he has done."
>
> ### Proverbs 19:17

📖 Please read Matthew 25:31–45. (In this story, the King represents Jesus Christ.) Explain how this parable illustrates Proverbs 19:17.

_____

_____

_____

I don't know about you, but the thought that when I give to the needs of others, I am essentially giving to Jesus humbles me. It reminds me of how many times I have ignored, refused, or simply missed the opportunity to give to Jesus by my lack of generosity.

📖 In the following proverbs note what wealth brings and what poverty allows:

Proverbs 10:15   wealth _____ poverty _____

Proverbs 13:8   wealth _____ poverty _____

Proverbs 14:20   wealth _____ poverty _____

Proverbs 19:4   wealth _____   poverty _____

Proverbs 22:7a   wealth _____   poverty _____

Proverbs 22:9   wealth _____   poverty _____

Proverbs 28:27   wealth _____   poverty _____

APPLY List the things you can do in your home, neighborhood, or community to help change what happens to the underprivileged?

_____

_____

_____

_____

Do you ever worry that if you give money to the poor that they will use it to continue in alcohol or drug addiction? I know I do. Years ago, my pastor commented he couldn't be in charge of our church benevolence fund, because he would "give away the store."

I believe that we need to be good stewards when we give to the poor. Check with your church and within your community for ways to help the needy so that your giving will truly bring benefits. But when in doubt about giving—give. Err on the side of grace, for God will honor your heart's mercy.

How would Proverbs 14:31 aid you in the decision to err on the side of giving too generously?

_____

_____

We find that when we give to the poor we honor God; that in and of itself should spur us on to freely give out of our material resources.

Read Proverbs 21:13 in the margin. What benefit do we derive from giving generously to others?

_____

_____

_____

Now let's examine an element of this proverb in a situation that occurred between Jesus and a wealthy young man. Please read Mark 10:17–23.

What did Jesus say to the wealthy young man (verse 21)?

_____

What was his reaction to Jesus' request (verse 22)?

_____

What did Jesus say to His disciples after the young man went away (verse 23)?

_____

Did you notice that it states, "Jesus looked at him and loved him?" But then Jesus requested that the young man sell everything and give the money to

"If a man shuts his ears to the cry of the poor, he too will cry out and not be answered."

Proverbs 21:13

the poor. The man's countenance fell in despair, because he couldn't let go of his wealth. Then Jesus made the profound statement, "How hard it is for the rich to enter the kingdom of God."

In your opinion, why do you think Jesus made this statement concerning the rich?

_____

_____

_____

📖 Read Luke 12:34 in the margin. How does this verse help explain Jesus' statement?

_____

_____

It is hard to believe and trust God, when we place our trust in our money. Human nature dictates that we will always love one more than the other.

Now consider the wealthy young man and Jesus in relationship to Proverbs 21:13. Prosperity has the potential to close up our hearts so that we can't hear God. It's not that He doesn't hear us, because Jesus heard the cry of the rich ruler, but the young man couldn't let go of his money in order to have his own questions answered or his prayer fulfilled.

 What of life's belongings, do you consider a treasure? If Jesus asked, could you leave this treasure behind to follow Jesus? Why or why not?

_____

_____

Today's Heart-Print
"He who is kind to the poor lends to the Lord, and he will reward him for what he has done." (Proverbs 19:17)

In closing, read Proverbs 30:8–10. Make it your closing prayer for today and continue to meditate on it the rest of the day.

Two things I ask of you, O Lord,

_____

_____

_____

_____

_____

_____

_____

"For where your treasure is, there your heart will be."
Luke 12:34

Extra Mile
LUKE 16:19–31

Review today's proverbs and then read Luke 16:19–31. Dissect the parable delivered in Luke and note any proverbs that would apply.

DESERT OF DEBT

Money is an article which may be used as a universal passport to everywhere except heaven, and as a universal provider of everything except happiness
—Anonymous[6]

"I am up to my neck in debt!" A recent television commercial for a credit-counseling agency shows scenes of a fashionable suburban man in his middle thirties, smiling happily as he sits astride a riding lawn mower while he brags about his possessions and his membership at the country club. Behind him, you spot a large, two-story home. A snazzy new vehicle sits polished in the driveway. The guy states proudly, "I am the envy of the neighborhood. How do I do it?" And then with a ridiculously plastered grin, he answers his own question: "I am in debt up to my eyeballs! Somebody help me!"

This guy didn't want to just keep up with the Joneses, he wanted to surpass them. However, his pride became detrimental.

The end of the commercial asks, "Are you in debt? We can help. Call us."

The commercial is quite humorous, but it conveys a sad truth about our society. Unfortunately, there are many of us Americans just like this goofy man, and just getting our finances in order will not solve our problems. Many of us need a heart transplant, from a heart of greed to a heart that values good stewardship with the monetary blessings already given by God.

How many people do you know that live beyond their earnings because they try to keep up with the Joneses? Can you relate to the stress involved in this type of situation? Living from paycheck to paycheck just to impress the neighbors? Arguing with your husband over money? Pasting a smile on your face as you whip out the credit card to buy the next unneeded item? Most of us can relate to buying more on credit than we should. Credit debt can destroy our finances, our marriages, and even our relationships with God.

Proverbs has much to say to those who take on debt and those who loan money to others to make an obscene profit. Here in Day Three, we are going to take a look at our spending. Ouch! I feel my toes being stepped on already!

📖 How would Proverbs 13:7 apply to the man in the commercial who said, "I am in debt up to my eyeballs!"?

_____

_____

_____

Although, in outward appearance it may appear he is wealthy, in reality he owns nothing. The truth is the bank and the credit card companies own him according to Proverbs 22:7.

📖 Read Proverbs 22:7

How would you define the second part of this proverb, *"the borrower is servant to the lender?"*

> **My Heart's Cry:**
>
> **Oh Lord, help me to free myself from the bondage of debt. Your Word teaches much in the area of borrowing money. Help me to apply the principles and concepts of learning to live within my income. In Jesus's name, Amen.**

> ## "The rich rule over the poor, and the borrower is servant to the lender."
>
> ### Proverbs 22:7

> ## "The wicked borrow and do not repay, but the righteous give generously."
>
> ### Psalm 37:21

Did You Know?
JUBILEE

In ancient Hebrew culture, God commanded that a Year of Jubilee be commemorated every fifty years. During this year of Jubilee, the land was not to be planted or harvested. The Israelites were supposed to gather and harvest only what the land produced spontaneously (see Leviticus 25:11–12). In addition, all land rented or sold reverted back to the original owners so that the property stayed within family lineage (Leviticus 25:13–34; 27:16–24). During this year of Jubilee all slaves were to be set free (Leviticus 25:39–54). It was to be a year of forgiven debts and a new beginning for those in debt.

I like *The Life Application Bible*'s explanation,

> Does this mean we should never borrow? No, but it warns us never to take on a loan without carefully examining our ability to repay it. A loan we can handle is enabling; a loan we can't handle is enslaving. The borrower must realize that until the loan is repaid, he or she is a servant to the individual or institution that made it.[7]

Debt in our society runs rampant. Recent news statistics report that the average American owes approximately nine thousand dollars on credit card debt alone. That plus, our mortgage and car loans put us at risk for bankruptcy. Bankruptcy is big business for attorneys. I searched the Internet for "bankruptcy law firms" and 297,634 popped up.

How does Psalm 37:21 describe someone who does not repay what they owe?

In the early New Testament era, filing bankruptcy was not an option. Read Matthew 18:23–34. Although this parable is a teaching on forgiveness, how does this describe the judicial system of the time concerning debt?

What warning did Jesus give in Matthew 5:25–26 that proves this point?

When Jesus lived on this earth, someone who couldn't pay a debt was thrown into prison until the debt was paid. Unless someone came to pay the debt for the prisoner, he or she would probably die there.[8]

Even if we have our debt under control, we still need to review some simple stewardship guidelines that we examined in Day One of this "Heart-Print of Finance" lesson.

Recently, I needed to sort through our belongings as we anticipated moving into a smaller home. "I feel like I am shopping at my own garage sale!" I murmured to myself. Sifting through closets, I discovered long-buried treasures. (Rather, treasures long-forgotten.) "Were they treasures if I didn't even remember them?" I pondered.

Moving-day hovered over my head. In two weeks, I needed these "treasures" boxed and ready to move into a smaller home. The question begged to be answered, "What in the world am I going to do with all this stuff?" Then a second question struck me. How much of this junk that I was about to toss or give away did I purchase on credit? Did I still owe money for something I no longer needed or even wanted?

I remember hearing the quip, "The second best day in a man's life is when he buys a new boat; the best is when he sells it." Yes, I can relate. Can you list a few things you now own that you wish you hadn't bought?

_____

_____

_____

In the margin read the proverbs from *The Message Bible* and then circle the advice that might apply to your household.

Now let's take a quick look at the flip side. Should *we* loan money and collect interest from others? Although few of us will loan money and expect to collect interest, let's examine a few other verses that deal with this monetary principle.

📖 Read the following verses and match the suggestion to the reference.

Exodus 22:25   Charge no interest to the needy

Deuteronomy 15:8   Beware of securing debt for someone else

Proverbs 11:15   Be openhanded and give freely

📖 Read the following verses from the New Testament and express what you think they teach.

Romans 13:8

_____

_____

Matthew 18:23–35

_____

_____

Matthew 25:16–27

_____

_____

Luke 7:41–43

_____

_____

John 2:13–17

_____

_____

> **"Whoever makes deals with strangers is sure to get burned; if you keep a cool head, you'll avoid rash bargains."**
>
> **Proverbs 11:15 (The Message)**

> **"It's stupid to try to get something for nothing, or run up huge bills you can never pay."**
>
> **Proverbs 17:18 (The Message)**

The following excerpt from *The International Standard Bible Encyclopedia* explains these verses in a more succinct manner than I can.

> The teaching of the New Testament on this subject is confined very largely to the parables of our Lord. Some think that the expression, "Owe no man anything" is an absolute warning against indebtedness. Quite a noticeable advance in the matter of debts and debtors is noticed as we enter the time of the New Testament. We read of bankers, exchangers, moneychangers, interest, investments, usury. The taking of

interest does not seem to be explicitly condemned in the New Testament . . . That compassion and leniency should be exercised toward those in debt is the clear teaching of Christ in the parables of the Unmerciful Servant and the Two Debtors.[9]

So, if we do choose to loan out money for profit what wisdom do you find in the following proverb?

"Hold tight to collateral on any loan to a stranger; be wary of accepting what a transient has pawned." (Proverbs 27:13; *The Message Bible*)

 Today's lesson ends with a quote from the apostle Paul. I feel it sums up today's lesson in a very succinct way. Read it carefully and close in a time of reflection and prayer.

"Give everyone what you owe him: If you owe taxes, pay taxes; if revenue, then revenue; if respect, then respect; if honor, then honor. Let no debt remain outstanding, except the continuing debt to love one another, for he who loves his fellowman has fulfilled the law." (Romans 13:7–8)

Today's Heart-Print
"The rich rule over the poor, and the borrower is servant to the lender."
(Proverbs 22:7)

Father God,

_____

_____

_____

_____

_____

_____

_____

_____

_____

Finances

DAY FOUR

"HI-HO! HI-HO! IT'S OFF TO WORK WE GO!"

It is not doing that which we like to do, but liking to do the thing which we have to do, that makes life blessed—Johann Wolfgang von Goethe.[10]

Whether we have a career, or just a job, or we are busy women who stay home, at times our work can feel like drudgery. I bet if you asked Tiger Woods about his golf career he would admit there are times he wished he'd chosen a different career path. But all work is part of life.

Here in Day Four, we are going take a review on why we work. Then more importantly, we will study how we should apply ourselves to work. What is our work ethic? Do we behave in a godly manner in our occupation?

With that thought in mind, I am reminded of Internet articles I have read over and over the past several weeks regarding employee behavior at work. Obviously, this topic holds huge importance. Let's delve into what the Word of God says about work. Today we are not going to start with Proverbs, but we will begin our study in the book that describes the early days of human labor. Now turn to Genesis, and let's begin.

Make a few notes about what you discover in the following verses:

Genesis 2:1–3

_____

_____

Genesis 2:15

_____

_____

Genesis 3:17–19

_____

_____

God worked. God rested. He instructed Adam to work and care for the Garden of Eden. This was before the Fall. Did you see that God instructed Adam and Eve to take care of the garden before they sinned? For years, I believed "work" was part of the curse of man. Work is not part of some curse, but the *toiling* of labor that is indicative of the curse of sin.

 Did you ever believe work was part of the curse? What is your view of labor now?

_____

_____

_____

Read Proverbs 14:23. What result does "all hard work" bring?

_____

_____

Hard works brings profits. I found the following statement amusing. I always give one hundred percent at work:

13% Monday

22% Tuesday

26% Wednesday

35% Thursday

4% Friday

I wish I could say I put forth the same effort on all days, but I don't. My different occupations have included several years in a variety of vocations, such as wife, office manager, stay-at-home mom, and a women's ministries director. What about you? Please list a few primary occupations that you have held.

My Heart's Cry:

Lord God, grant me the grace to work at whatever I do as if I am working for You. Whether I am working in an office, a store, or cleaning my home, I want to do the best job possible. Help me work with integrity and cheerfulness. In Your precious name, Amen.

"All hard work brings a profit, but mere talk leads only to poverty."

Proverbs 14:23

Word Study
WORK

One Hebrew word sometimes translated in our Bibles as "work" is *itstsabon,* which refers to pain or toil. It occurs three times in Genesis alone relating to the curse that God placed on fallen humanity. To the woman, God stated that she would have pain and toil during childbirth (see Genesis 3:16). To the man, God stated, that he would have pain and toil in working the ground to produce food (see Genesis 3:17; 5:29).[11]

"Whatever you do, work at it with all your heart, as working for the Lord, not for men."

Colossians 3:23

1. _____
2. _____
3. _____
4. _____
5. _____

APPLY What does Colossians 3:23 mean in your day-to-day life?

_____
_____
_____

If we want to share our faith at work, how would Colossians 3:23 explain the following saying? "Monday religion is better than Sunday profession."

_____
_____

📖 Even though we may attend church every Sunday, our behavior at work speaks louder to others than anything "religious" we might say or do. Now let's dig into some proverbs on this topic. They hold quite a bit of proverbial knowledge to instill in us concerning our work ethic. Jot down what they advise.

Proverbs 12:11

_____

Proverbs 12:14

_____

Proverbs 18:9

_____

Proverbs 21:25

_____

Can you see that God highly values a good work ethic? He expects us to provide for our families and ourselves. Which of the above proverbs spoke most profoundly to you? Why?

_____
_____
_____

How would your interpret Proverbs 22:29 and 27:18?

_____
_____
_____
_____

Being diligent and skilled in our work is the best way to influence an employer. Diligence often results in a promotion. Hearing about a good worker, an employer may want to promote him or give other extra rewards.

However, a primary principle we must remember, we work as to the Lord, not to men. Let's look again at Colossians 3:22–25 from *The Message* Bible.

> *Servants, do what you're told by your earthly masters. And don't just do the minimum that will get you by. Do your best. Work from the heart for your real Master, for God, confident that you'll get paid in full when you come into your inheritance. Keep in mind always that the ultimate Master you're serving is Christ. The sullen servant who does shoddy work will be held responsible. Being Christian doesn't cover up bad work.*

What would be the opposite response to *"being a Christian doesn't cover up bad work?"*

_____

_____

As Christians, we should be diligent in our vocations and strive for excellence. We shouldn't be sloppy or deceitful in any way, but instead we must act with honesty and integrity. Let's see what certain proverbs have to say on these topics.

📖 Read the following verses and then write down a brief description of each.

Proverbs 10:2

_____

_____

_____

Proverbs 10:9

_____

_____

_____

Proverbs 11:1, 3

_____

_____

_____

Proverbs 11:18, 20

_____

_____

_____

Proverbs 13:4

_____

_____

_____

"Do you see a man skilled in his work? He will serve before kings; he will not serve before obscure men."

Proverbs 22:29

"He who tends a fig tree will eat its fruit, and he who looks after his master will be honored."

Proverbs 27:18

Proverbs 13:13

_____

_____

_____

Proverbs 15:6

_____

_____

_____

Proverbs 16:8

_____

_____

_____

Proverbs 20:4

_____

_____

_____

APPLY All right, now let's take a look at our own honesty and integrity in the workplace. Place an X by any unethical activities you have committed that essentially robbed your employer.

☐ called in sick though not ill   ☐ took long lunches
☐ took paperclips, pencils, etc.   ☐ chatted by the coffee pot
☐ added time to your time card   ☐ browsed the Internet for personal use
☐ made personal phone calls   ☐ padded your expenses account

Read the following proverbs and then rank them in the order of those that resemble your life the most (#1 being the most relevant).

"Go to the ant, you sluggard; consider its ways and be wise! It has no commander, no overseer or ruler, yet it stores its provisions in summer and gathers its food at harvest." (Proverbs 6:6–8)

"The laborer's appetite works for him; his hunger drives him on." (Proverbs 16:26)

"Finish your outdoor work and get your fields ready; after that, build your house." (Proverbs 24:27)

Usually our needs drive us to make the most of our time and our money. Only then do we begin to budget and plan for our financial future.

APPLY How could Proverbs 21:20 apply to retirement in modern times? What are you doing to prepare for old age and retirement?

_____

_____

_____

Proverbs 21:20 advises us to save and store up for future needs. It is a foolish man who spends all he earns without saving. Review with the Lord today your work ethic and your spending habits. Pray for Him to show you clear direction in both areas.

Today's Heart-Print
"Whatever you do, work at it with all your heart, as working for the Lord, not for men." (Colossians 3:23)

My Master, my God,

_____

_____

_____

_____

_____

_____

_____

_____

WHO'S THE BOSS?

Finances

DAY FIVE

Nothing so conclusively proves a man's ability to lead others as what he does from day to day to lead himself—Thomas J. Watson[12]

"This is the longest I have ever held a job," Sheryl remarked smugly. After working for my husband's company for seven weeks, she felt secure in her position. However, her poor work habits, ditzy attitudes, and not to mention cockroaches falling out of her handbag (I'm serious!), were cause for my husband, Mark, to let her go.

I nodded and looked at the floor. By 5:00 p.m., she would be looking for another job.

My husband struggles each time he needs to fire someone. Although, he has been an employer for over twenty-five years the decision and action to terminate an employee plagues him for days.

A couple of years ago, he needed to let someone else go for numerous reasons. Finally, one night at dinner he announced he would tell her the next day that it was her last day to work for him.

I said, "Mark, it's the day before Christmas Eve. You can't do that!"

He looked surprised and said, "You're right, I can't." He's not unkind; he just wasn't thinking about the Christmas season while considering what to do about his employee. Being a boss is hard. So whether we are employed as peons or executives, I hope our Day Five study helps us to understand the position of authority. Let's evaluate what levels of authority you may have attained in life. Place an X by the position that has been assigned to you at some point in your life.

❑ mother   ❑ caretaker of aging parents
❑ ministry position   ❑ employer or manager in workforce
❑ community leadership   ❑ teacher
❑ other _____

📖 Now's let's read a few proverbs. Today's lesson approach is a little different from the usual one where we look up the verses. I am using *The Message* Bible for several of the verses we look at in Day Five, because I think its modern language will help our understanding in leadership. (*The Message* Bible translates the terms *king* and *ruler* as *leader*.) Please examine the following proverbs as quoted from *The Message* and then underline positive traits of a good leader. Circle negative actions of someone in leadership. Then give an example of each verse that could apply to yourself and to a leadership position you hold.

Proverbs 16:10: *"A good leader motivates, doesn't mislead, doesn't exploit."*

_____

_____

Proverbs 16:12–13: *"Good leaders abhor wrongdoing of all kinds; sound leadership has a moral foundation. Good leaders cultivate honest speech; they love advisors who tell them the truth."*

_____

_____

Proverbs 20:8: *"Leaders who know their business and care keep a sharp eye out for the shoddy and cheap."*

_____

_____

Proverbs 20:26: *"After careful scrutiny, a wise leader makes a clean sweep of rebels and dolts."*

_____

_____

Proverbs 20:28: *"Love and truth form a good leader; sound leadership is founded on loving integrity."*

_____

_____

Proverbs 22:11: *"God loves the pure-hearted and well-spoken; good leaders also delight in their friendship."*

_____

_____

Proverbs 29:4: *"A leader of good judgment gives stability; an exploiting leader leaves a trail of waste."*

My Heart's Cry:

Lord, I am often put in a position of authority. Whether I am disciplining my children, teaching Sunday school, or serving as the CEO of a corporation, give me the wisdom to guide with a godly heart. Keep my work ethics pure and unselfish. Amen.

_____

_____

Proverbs 29:14: *"Leadership gains authority and respect when the voiceless poor are treated fairly."*

_____

_____

These proverbs state clearly that we will gain respect when we treat others fairly. But most important, we need a loving and pure heart filled with integrity. We need to watch for shoddy work but compliment those who do a good job and work hard.

📖 In the margin, what does Proverbs 14:35 tell us about commending someone?

_____

_____

Mark Twain once said, "I can live for two months on a good compliment." Whom in your life could you compliment today on their attitudes or accomplishments? (Think of anyone whom your leadership influences.)

_____

_____

📖 Of course, compliments are wonderful, but the Word of God expects something else from employers. Read the following verses and note what each says about wages.

Deuteronomy 24:14–15

_____

_____

Leviticus 19:13

_____

_____

Jeremiah 22:13

_____

_____

1 Timothy 5:18

_____

_____

Scripture clearly states that as employers we are to pay fair wages for the work others provide for us. We shouldn't hoard the profits for ourselves, but give each man his due work.

📖 Now read James 5:4. What does this verse state about those we fail to pay for their toil?

> **"Diligent work gets a warm commendation; shiftless work earns an angry rebuke."**
>
> **Proverbs 14:35 (The Message)**

_____

_____

This verse rebukes those who live in luxury and indulgence at the expense of their laborers. God notices what we do as employers. Let's make sure that we pay fair wages to the people who work for us.

Now let's close with one more area concerning our work ethics and leadership roles.

📖 Please read Exodus 20:10–11. What does this verse instruct us to do?

_____

_____

APPLY Do you remember when we read in Genesis that God rested on the seventh day? Of course, in the United States we have grown accustomed to a five-day work week and usually some vacation time. However, what about ourselves? Whether you are self-employed, a mom, or any type of workaholic, do you give yourself time to rest? Why or why not?

_____

_____

_____

📖 Read Leviticus 23:3.

Write your definition of the term, "Sabbath."

_____

_____

_____

For myself, I think of _rest_ when I hear the term "Sabbath." There is nothing I like better than a Sunday afternoon nap. It refreshes and replenishes my energy for the beginning of the next work-week. Let's look at the meaning of "Sabbath" from a Bible expert's perspective.

> The sabbath is a sacred and Divine institution; a privilege and benefit, not a task and drudgery. God never designed it to be a burden to us, therefore we must not make it so to ourselves. The sabbath was instituted for the good of mankind, as living in society, having many wants and troubles, preparing for a state of happiness or misery. Man was not made for the sabbath, as if his keeping it could be of service to God, nor was he commanded to keep it outward observances to his real hurt. Every observance respecting it, is to be interpreted by the rule of mercy.[12]

APPLY Do you make time to spend a Sabbath time with God? Why or why not?

_____

_____

_____

How did Jesus explain a Sabbath in the following verses?

Mark 2:27

_____

Mark 3:4

_____

In closing, describe what you have learned about leadership today. Think back a few years, consider your position now and anticipate your future. Write a prayer asking God to help you in leadership in all areas of your life.

Today's Heart-Print
"Love and truth form a good leader; sound leadership is founded on loving integrity." (Proverbs 20:28 *The Message*)

Lord God,

_____

_____

_____

_____

_____

_____

_____

_____

_____

Your Heart's Impression

Journal your thoughts about learning wisdom regarding the financial aspects of your life.

_____

_____

_____

_____

Describe your thoughts about your own generosity to others.

_____

_____

_____

_____

Write your thoughts about debt and what God's Word tells us:

_____

_____

_____

Journal how you feel about your work ethic.

_____

_____

_____

_____

Explain how and why you will begin to take a rest from your work schedule on a regular basis.

_____

_____

_____

_____

Tell the Lord God what is in your heart after this lesson.

Lord,

_____

_____

_____

_____

_____

1. Frank S. Mead, *12,000 Religious Quotations*, (Grand Rapids, MI: Baker Book House, 1989), 427.

2. Ibid., 311.

3. Ronald. J. Sider, *Rich Christians In An Age of Hunger* (Waco, TX: W Publishing Group, 1997), 1–37.

4. *Scripture Press Publications,* Licensed by Victor Books. In NavPress Software Database, © 1997.

5. Max Anders, *Holman Old Testament Commentary-Proverbs* (Nashville,TN: Holman Reference, 2005), *276.*

6. Mead, *12,000 Religious Quotations*, 309.

7. *Life Application Bible* (Wheaton, IL: Tyndale House Publishers, Inc., 1991). In NavPress Software Database, © 1997.

8. Ibid.

9. *International Standard Bible Encyclopedia*. In NavPress Software Database, © 1998.

10. Mead, *12,000 Religious Quotations*, 473.

11. http://thinkexist.com/quotes/thomas_j._watson,_sr./.

12. Matthew Henry, *Concise Commentary* in WORDsearch Bible software. CD-ROM, 2003

13. Warren Baker, D.R.E. and Eugene Carpenter, Ph.D.; eds. *The Complete Word Study Dictionary Old Testament* (Chattanooga, TN: AMG Publishers, 2003).

Heart-Print of Time

What then is time? If no one asks me, I know what it is. If I wish to explain it to him who asks, I do not know.—Saint Augustine[1]

Who are we eternally?" "Inside I am still the essence of the little boy I was sixty-five years ago," stated Professor Stock. He held the attention of the undergraduate philosophy class. He went on to explain that even though time passes, the basis of who we are doesn't change. We grow into mature adults, but at any given moment we can suddenly peer out from our souls from the same sense of perspective we entertained as a child.

I understood his theory because the smell of sagebrush on a hot summer day transports me immediately back to playing house in the foothills behind my childhood home. In the fall when leaves crunch underfoot, I recall walking in the brisk wind to elementary school. I am still that little girl.

In this week's lesson we will study various aspects of time. As we do this, we will focus on God's perspective of time and attempt to understand how we use time to benefit God's kingdom.

Although we will study the Book of Proverbs (as always), we will also look closely at the Book of Ecclesiastes. Proverbs and Ecclesiastes, both written by Solomon, fall into the category of what is considered "Wisdom Literature." Since the theory of *time* confuses most us, we'll examine it from several biblical perspectives and attempt to understand what time means to us each day. So let's not waste any more time!

In this week's lesson we will study various aspects of time. As we do this, we will focus on God's perspective of time and attempt to understand how we use time to benefit God's kingdom.

IN THE BEGINNING

Always remember that the future comes one day at a time.—Dean Acheson[2]

My Heart's Cry:

My Creator, this earth amazes me. Today give me the ability to grasp the concept of what time is within Your creation. Enable me to use my time for the good of Your eternal purpose. In Your name, Amen.

The idea of time travel fascinates people. The 1980s film *Back to the Future* entertained and stretched our imaginations as to the "what ifs" of going back in time. The lead character, Marty Mcfly, travels backwards in time. He changes history inadvertently and prevents his parents from meeting. No meeting of Mom and Dad, results in no birth of Marty McFly. McFly realizes the dilemma and attempts throughout the movie to rectify his mistake. Of course, he achieves his goal. Mcfly then travels back to modern time with the knowledge of what might have been.

If we could travel back in time, we might discover the answer to some of the world's most perplexing questions. What did happen to the dinosaurs? Which came first, the chicken or the egg? Well we can't answer those questions, but we are going back in time—to the very beginning.

📖 Read Genesis 1:1. Write down the first five words. What do you discover within these five words?

_____

_____

_____

"In the beginning God created. . . ." These words, in a sense, allow us the opportunity to experience time travel. We can visualize the very beginning of time, as God created time before He created the universe. God existed before time. He is timeless. Let's take a moment to see how God defines Himself.

📖 Read Exodus 3:13–15.

It makes me smile to visualize a barefoot Moses quaking before a burning bush, and that he had the audacity to inquire as to God's name. God replied with the declaration, "I AM Who I AM." This expression of "I AM" is the Hebrew word *YHWH*. When pronounced it sounded as "Yahweh." We now translate *YHWH* as "Jehovah." The Jews have long revered the name "Jehovah." Out of reverence for the name "Jehovah," to this day, when they read the Scriptures aloud, they exchange YHWH with the Hebrew word for "Lord": *Adonai*.

📖 Now I want us to review another section of Scripture in the New Testament. Please read John 18:3–8.

With what words did Jesus acknowledge Himself?

_____

_____

_____

Describe what happened to the band of men who came to arrest Jesus when He spoke these words (Verse 6).

Extra Mile
GENESIS AND PROVERBS

Read all of Genesis 1. Compare it to Proverbs 8:12, 22–31. Note the similarities and the differences. Now read John 1. Whom do you think Proverbs referred to as "Wisdom" in Proverbs 8?

_____

_____

📖 Read Mark 14:60–64. Again how does Jesus describe Himself, and what reaction follows His statement?

_____

_____

_____

He says, "I am he." These words are translated from the Greek word, *eimi,* meaning *"I exist"* or *"I am."* Jesus likely spoke these words in Aramaic, and those who heard Him recognized that He declared Himself to be God. The men in the garden staggered to remain on their feet from the power those simple words brought forth. The Jewish leaders in the Sanhedrin considered the statement blasphemy and worthy of execution.

📖 Read the following verses and note the description given for God.

Genesis 21:33

_____

Psalm 102:27

_____

Isaiah 40:28

_____

Hebrews 13:8

_____

Revelation 1:8

_____

Revelation 21:6

_____

Revelation 22:13

_____

God transcends the boundaries of time. He exists as self-existing and self-defining. He is the Everlasting, The Beginning and the End. As the Lord of time He created it and defined it. Mind boggling isn't it? Even such brilliant minds as Albert Einstein's and Steven Hawking's can only surmise what time is. So we are not going to tackle the theories of time and relativity (aren't you thankful?), but we are going to research how the Bible refers to the mystery of time.

The word "time" or "times" appears on approximately nine hundred occasions in English translations of the Bible. "Time" can be translated many ways in the Hebrew. The word has many synonyms in English alone. List as many words as you can that relate to a period of time. I will start you with three examples:

"Jesus Christ is the same yesterday and today and forever."

Hebrews 13:8

Extra Mile
TIME

God is the Lord of time. Read Joshua 10:12–14 and 2 Kings 20:1–11. What happened with time in these accounts? For what purpose did God change time for Joshua and Hezekiah?

day, hour, moment,_____

_____

_____

_____

"I am the Alpha and the Omega, the First and the Last, the Beginning and the End."

Revelation 22:13

📖 The Bible also uses different words to refer to a segment of time. Match the following proverbs with the correct synonym for *time*.

Proverbs 3:2	future
Proverbs 3:28	times
Proverbs 7:9	season
Proverbs 12:19	moment
Proverbs 20:4	day/night
Proverbs 23:18	tomorrow
Proverbs 24:10	years

One thing we can learn from Day One is that regardless of how we describe various segments of time, we know God does not change with or over time. He is the Beginning and the End, the Alpha and the Omega, the I AM.

As we close Day One, lets mediate on the eternal greatness of our God. Please read and then paraphrase Psalm 93. Use this as your closing prayer of praise to the Lord God Almighty, Jesus Christ.

Today's Heart-Print
"Do you not know? Have you not heard? The Lord is the everlasting God, the Creator of the ends of the earth. He will not grow tired or weary, and his understanding no one can fathom." (Isaiah 40:28)

Lord God,

_____

_____

_____

_____

_____

_____

Time

DAY TWO

ONCE UPON A TIME

How we spend our days is, of course, how we spend our lives
—Annie Dillard[3]

Children's stories often begin with the phrase, *"Once upon a time."* It gives the clue that what we are about to read is fiction. The tale often depicts a damsel in distress as a result of some unexpected conflict in her life. The climactic conclusion usually ends with the hero riding in on a white horse to rescue the maiden from peril. And predictably, the story concludes with a nice tidy ending such as, *"And they lived happily ever after."*

If only the narrative of our lives could be so easily told. If only we knew what the future holds. And of course, we desire our own, *"They lived happily ever after,"* knowing that we can only hope for the best and fear the worst. The future remains an unknown.

Although we believe we would like to see into our future, it would not benefit us in most cases. I recall a psychology teacher once stating, "If we could know our futures, it would drive us insane." What if we could see all the joy before us, but also the tragedies? Most likely, the foreboding sorrow would dominate our thoughts.

With today's medical technology we see doors opening to look into the future of our health. Already some people can decide to test for what their inherited genes hold in store for them. These tests determine their likelihood of developing cancer, heart disease, Alzheimer's disease, and other catastrophic illnesses. Many people who could test for a devastating illness choose not to. Why? Because they don't want to know.

God in His divine wisdom and sovereignty limits our knowledge of the future. However, He does advise us that good times and bad times will be a part of everyone's life. Today let's look at how the Bible expresses life in the real world.

📖 Read Proverbs 27:1. Summarize what this verse states.

_____

_____

📖 With Proverbs 27:1 still in mind, read Ecclesiastes 3:1–8. As you read, correlate circumstances that have occurred in your life with each verse. How would Proverbs 27:1 apply to each?

verse 2

_____

_____

_____

verse 3

_____

_____

_____

verse 4

_____

_____

_____

verse 5

_____

_____

My Heart's Cry:

Father, I know life holds joy and happiness, pain and sorrow. Help me appreciate the good times and grant grace to uphold me in the difficult seasons of life. Help me to remember You are the God of both. In Jesus' name, Amen.

"Do not boast about tomorrow, for you do not know what a day may bring forth."

Proverbs 27:1

verse 6

_____

_____

verse 7

_____

_____

verse 8

_____

_____

Within the past five years, I have experienced much of what Ecclesiastes 3:1–8 states. I mourned the death of my father and my mother-in-law. The birth of my first granddaughter caused my feet to dance, and I heartily embraced a new daughter-in-law and at the same time gave up my son to marriage. I wept at the sight of devastation from the tsunami that swept across much of Asia. It has been a time of war in Iraq, but a time of peace in my own home.

📖 What does each of the following proverbs imply?

Proverbs 24:10

_____

_____

Proverbs 25:19

_____

_____

On the scale below, note how much, if at all, you falter in times of trouble.

⬅──────────────────────────────────────➡

I never fall   I trip, but catch myself   I skin my knees   I fall flat on my face

I don't know about you, but I usually falter in times of difficulty. I stumble with my faith in God and ask, "Why me?" I tend to look for other people to strengthen me, but many times they are unreliable or unable to uphold me. But there is good news for the likes of us who need a little hand up every now again.

📖 What do the following verses assure us?

Psalm 27:5

_____

_____

Psalm 46:1

_____

_____

"There is a time for everything, and a season for every activity under heaven."

**Ecclesiastes 3:1**

Psalm 50:15

_____

_____

Although our vigor may fail, we can receive strength in the Lord. He will catch us, if we call upon Him when life's troubles surge over us. He will set our feet on a firm foundation, so that we will not be shaken. God will be our strength no matter what the future holds.

What meaning can you derive from Proverbs 16:3–4, 9?

_____

_____

_____

Compare these verses to Proverbs 21:30–31.

_____

_____

_____

How does Roman 8:28 apply to both of these passages?

_____

_____

_____

The verses in Proverbs 16 instruct us to plan for the future. Yet, Proverbs 21 warns us that as we plan, we must understand that the ultimate course of our life is set by the Lord. So even as we chart the direction of our desires, we must realize that God ultimately works out everything according to His purpose for us. He always works in our best interests with an eternal perspective. How does 1 Peter 5:10 sum up the ultimate goal of God when the "the day of trouble arrives?"

_____

_____

In God's perspective when we face a season of suffering, it helps to make us strong, firm, and steadfast. He restores and upholds with His strength, not ours. It would behoove us to remember 1 Peter 5:10 when troubled times come.

In Day Two, we have observed that our time here on earth will probably not be a "Once upon a time" type of story. Days of trouble will happen in the future for each of us. At times we will be damsels in distress, but remember the eternal perspective of God. He will come to our rescue and strengthen us.

According to Revelation 19:10–16 who will come forth riding on a white horse for us someday in the future?

_____

_____

The hero we will see will be Jesus Christ riding on a white horse with the title, "King of Kings and Lord of Lords." Can you shout, Hallelujah? He will come as our hero and king. Do you realize at the end of time we will truly be able to say, "And they lived happily ever after." Hallelujah!

 Now take a few moments to meditate Today's Heart-Print. Let's spend some time in prayer and praise. Praise Him for the seasons of joy and happiness that flood your life. Ask Jesus to strengthen you when times of distress strike. Rejoice and thank Him for being your King on a white horse who will always uphold you.

Today's Heart-Print
"There is a time for everything, and a season for every activity under heaven."
(Ecclesiastes 3:1)

Lord Jesus,

_____

_____

_____

_____

_____

_____

_____

_____

_____

Time

TIME'S A WASTING

Time is what we want most, but what we use worst—William Penn[4]

According to the old fable, a grasshopper hopped about in a field one summer's day, chirped, and sang to its heart's content. An ant passed by, bearing along with great toil an ear of corn. He struggled to drag it home.

"Why not come and sing with me," said the grasshopper, "instead of working so hard in the heat of the day."

"I am helping my fellow ants to lay up food for the coming winter," said the ant, "and recommend for you to do the same."

"Who cares about winter?" said the grasshopper; "I have plenty of food today." But the ant went on its way, working diligently. When winter came, the grasshopper had no food or provision and found itself dying of hunger, while it saw ants distributing corn everyday from the provision they had stored up in the summer. Then the grasshopper knew he had been lazy and not prepared for the days ahead.

Of course the moral of the story is that we are to make the most of our time.

The fable, "The Ant and the Grasshopper," relates a general moral truth. Aesop, a Greek slave, taught the story to others around 550 BC, along with numerous other fables. Many fables have parallels to the Proverbs of the Bible. So let's see what we can learn from the ant today.

Compare the fable of The *Ant and the Grasshopper* to Proverbs 6:6–8.

_____

_____

_____

What similarities did you find?

_____

_____

What is the moral of this story?

_____

_____

_____

APPLY Both the fable and this proverb discuss the diligence of the ant. The ant because of hard work in the summer has ample provision in the winter. The messages of both the proverb and the fable challenge us to work hard and prepare for the future. Unfortunately, I enjoy lazing around in the summer. How about you? What are a few of your favorite summer activities?

_____

_____

_____

I like to sit outside and read. Eating a slice of chilled crispy watermelon underneath a shade tree relaxes me. I enjoy going to a beach and watching the waves bounce little children into the sand. Who wants to slave away in the heat? Though periods of rest and relaxation are essential to our existence, we can learn from the grasshopper that it isn't wise to relax all the time.

📖 Read Proverbs 24:30–34

What lesson did Solomon learn as evidenced in this proverb?

_____

_____

_____

What questions does Proverbs 6:9–10 ask the sluggard?

_____

_____

_____

My Heart's Cry:

Dear Lord, teach me to utilize my time in the most efficient way to benefit Your kingdom. Help me to plan for the future, but also, to live for today. Guide me toward achieving Your purpose in my life. Do not let me become lazy, but remind me to put forth my best effort in all my tasks.

The word "sluggard" refers to someone sluggish, lazy, or useless. Christians who are slothful have little or no success in ministering to others. They are not goal-oriented, and their lives are not productive. These people take no initiative and do not get tasks done on time. They tend to do little work and create imaginary excuses for their laziness.[5]

I don't know about you, but I love to sleep. If allowed, I would sleep ten hours a night and then take a nice nap in the afternoon. However, life doesn't afford me the luxury to sleep as much as I would like. Appointments, deadlines, and daily activities keep me from snoozing. I believe I could be a sluggard if permitted. What about you, how much sleep do you get?

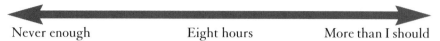

Never enough   Eight hours   More than I should

Although we need to have enough sleep, the point of these proverbs is not to waste time by oversleeping. Of course, there are other ways we can be sluggards besides oversleeping.

 Circle the activities where you might waste time on average day. Add other time-wasters that might come to your mind.

surfing the Internet	shopping
TV	crafts
talking on the phone	computer games

The above activities are not wrong in and of themselves as outlets for relaxation and leisure. However if we consistently fill our time doing these things, then we need to ask God to help us make some healthy adjustments. For example, I used to play the card game of Hearts on the computer for hours at a time. As a writer, I should have been working at the computer; whenever I felt a "writer's block" coming on, I would switch the screen to play Hearts. Hours would pass and not a page would be written. I finally deleted Hearts off of my computer, but then I chose to play Solitaire. That card game eventually went to the computer's recycle bin, too. I couldn't conduct myself with moderation with Hearts or Solitaire when it was just a click away. It required complete abstinence.

I like how *The Message* states Proverbs 26:13–16. Make a note of what behavioral traits you see in the sluggard mentioned in these verses:

> *"Loafers say, 'It's dangerous out there! Tigers are prowling the streets!' and then pull the covers back over their heads. Just as a door turns on its hinges, so a lazybones turns back over in bed. A shiftless sluggard puts his fork in the pie, but is too lazy to lift it to his mouth.*
>
> *Dreamers fantasize their self-importance; they think they are smarter than a whole college faculty."*

 Sluggards consider themselves wise. They feel important even when it is apparent that laziness rules their activities. Plus, they make excuses for lack of work. Do you know anyone like this? What about you? Do you make excuses to get out of work?

_____

_____

_____

_____

_____

📖 Read Proverbs 10:26.

Can you think of a word or two to describe how a lazy person affects someone else?

Sluggards are annoying. They rub us the wrong way. OK, enough about sluggards for the moment. Let's look at another type of person—the diligent one.

📖 Read Proverbs 27:23–27. Let's strain our brains. Rewrite this proverb with activities that are relevant for today's culture.

_____

_____

_____

_____

This list could include anything that fills our time and produces a benefit. My husband doesn't tend to a flock of sheep, but he does sell insurance to provide for our family. We pay our bills, purchase groceries, and sustain ourselves in many other ways as a result.

Let's study a man who worked diligently and benefited from the results.

📖 Read Genesis 41:46–57

Describe what Joseph did during the seven years of abundance?

_____

_____

_____

What happened during the seven years of famine?

_____

_____

📖 How would each of the following proverbs apply to Joseph's diligence?

Proverbs 10:4

_____

_____

Proverbs 12:24

_____

_____

Proverbs 12:27

_____

_____

Proverbs 13:4

_____

_____

Proverbs 21:5

_____

_____

Joseph worked hard for all of the seven years of abundance. He didn't sit back after a year or two of prosperity; he kept on harvesting the grain. Then when the famine and hard times hit, not only was he prepared, but he also continued to work and to benefit: *"And all the countries came to Egypt to buy grain from Joseph because the famine was severe in all the world"* (Genesis 41:57).

 So do you consider yourself diligent like Joseph, or are you a loafer? In actuality, most of us are probably a little of both. The goal of today's lesson is to make us aware of our shortcomings in time management. Take a few minutes, (no this isn't wasting time), to ask God's help in being more diligent in your use of time.

Today's Heart-Print
"The sluggard craves and gets nothing, but the desires of the diligent are fully satisfied." (Proverbs 13:4)

Lord God,

_____

_____

_____

_____

_____

_____

_____

_____

_____

_____

> "Diligent hands will rule, but laziness ends in slave labor."
>
> **Proverbs 12:24**

Time

DAY FOUR

PRICELESS MOMENTS

But what minutes! Count them by sensation, and not by calendars, and each moment is a day.—Benjamin Disraeli[6]

Time seems to drag by for children. They wait impatiently for their next birthday to come. Summertime lasts forever. At the beginning of September, nine months of school manifests itself as an eternity. An eight-hour car ride takes forever. "Are we there yet, Mom?"

As adults, we can't believe another candle stands atop our birthday cake. Summer flies by. Didn't we just box up the Christmas ornaments? Why do we hear "Jingle Bells" on the radio already?

Why does time appear to move at different speeds when we're young or old? One reason is children focus on the now. They are totally in their moment of action, no matter what they are doing. Adults tend to focus on the future. We develop more complex thought processes to understand the passing of time. We look to the future and worry about "we don't have enough time."

In ancient time, the Greeks could express the difference between **actual time** and **perceived time.** They used two words to describe the concept of time, *chrónos* and *kairós* (pronounced ky-ros). *Chrónos* is clock time. Our English word *chronological* is derived from *chrónos*. It is how we measure time in the real world. *Chrónos* is time we are aware of. Consider how we become anxious waiting for the surgeon's report on our loved one. The hands of the clock tick-tock slowly until the doctor walks down the hallway with a smile on his face. Chrónos time is analytical and real time.

Children tend to live more in the other concept of time (*kairós*). *Kairós* time is the dimension of time we become absorbed into. It's those moments when we are unaware that time has passed by. When we engage in activities that bring us joy or that we are passionate about, we are in the dimension of *kairós* time. Like when we chat with our girlfriend and it seems like only a few minutes have passed, but then we look at our watches (*chrónos* or actual time) and realize that two hours have passed. It is the difference of studying for your least favorite subject in school or reading a book from the best-seller list. One activity feels as if time drags, while you become so absorbed in the other that you are completely unaware of time passing.

Although adults perceive time as going by quickly, we can relearn a child-like perception of time. We should slow down in our thinking to recognize and appreciate priceless moments of time.

 Please mark how time passes for you during these happenings. Place an F next to occasions that seem to fly by or a D when time drags. Mark those that appear to fly and drag at the same time with an FD.

__ having the flu __ your day off
__ vacations __ a car accident
__ raising children __ visiting relatives
__ Monday at work __ rollercoaster rides
__ Thanksgiving dinner __ Christmas morning
__ rush hour traffic __ pregnancy
__ the school year __ summer

Of course, our answers will vary from person to person. It will depend on how much we enjoy the activity (or the visiting relative!). But I think we could all agree when we have the flu, the clock hardly moves. Do you see how our attitudes about time are able to twist and turn according to our circumstances?

Read Proverbs 24:10 along with Job 4:5. What does it state might happen during slow, difficult seasons of life?

_____

_____

_____

In contrast, what does Proverbs 24:16 imply?

_____

_____

My Heart's Cry:

Lord, I realize that I race through life and miss priceless moments each day. Give me eyes to see the bright florescent rainbow. Instead of annoyance, remind me to listen joyfully to the morning song chirped by the birds outside my window. Make me aware of life! Thank You, Lord.

Discouragement, distress, and depression stalk my heart when hard times hit, and these feelings always seem to linger for a while. What happens to you when time moves slowly through laborious seasons of life?

As we have seen, time can seem to move differently for various reasons. Now let's look at time from a "God perspective." What do you learn from the following verses?

Psalm 90:4

_____

_____

2 Peter 3:8

_____

_____

Would you describe these examples as illustrations of *chrónos* or *kairós*?

_____

_____

Remember that *kairós* time doesn't necessarily appear chronological. I believe both of these verses refer to *kairós*.

Let's look at a situation in Exodus that seems to express the difference in time based on our perceptions of time and God's perspective.

📖 Read Exodus 32:1–8.

How did the people perceive time? (verse 1)

_____

_____

What did the Lord say about the time frame? (verse 8)

_____

_____

The Israelites experienced the feeling that Moses had been gone a long time.

> *When the people saw that Moses was so long in coming down from the mountain they gathered around Aaron. . . . "As for this fellow Moses who brought us up out of Egypt we don't know what has happened to him." (Exodus 32:1)*

But the Lord's perspective differed, *"Then the LORD said to Moses. . . . They have been quick to turn away from what I have commanded of them"* (Exodus 32:7–8).

So we see that time differs in perspective based on who is looking, and how he is looking. The Bible gives us several glimpses into the reality of how short life is in comparison to eternity.

📖 Read the following verses. Give the description given of our lives.

Job 7:7a

_____

_____

_____

Psalm 39:5

_____

_____

_____

Psalm 144:4

_____

_____

_____

James 4:14b

_____

_____

_____

Our lives evaporate like the mist. Our time here on earth is short. How should we spend our time according to Ecclesiastes 11:8?

📖 Read Ecclesiastes 11:8 in the margin and then fill in the blanks below.

_"However_____ a man may live, let him _____

Do you know what Sam Butcher is famous for? Mr. Butcher designs teardrop-eyed children figurines. He captures the youngsters involved in endearing poses of everyday life. The poses evoke a tender response from our hearts. These small pastel statues are known as "Precious Moments."® For over three decades, customers have purchased these adorable collectables to remind themselves of time's treasured moments.

Examine the following proverbs to note the wisdom they offer concerning the priceless moments of our life.

"You don't want to squander your wonderful life, to waste your precious life among the hardhearted." (Proverbs 5:9; _The Message_)

"Mark a life of discipline and live wisely; don't squander your precious life." (Proverbs 8:33; _The Message_)

"It's through me, Lady Wisdom, that your life deepens, and the years of your life ripen." (Proverbs 9:11; _The Message_)

"A miserable heart means a miserable life; a cheerful heart fills the day with song." (Proverbs 15:15; _The Message_)

"Life, lovely while it lasts, is soon over. Life as we know it, precious and beautiful, ends." (Ecclesiastes 12:6; _The Message_)

> **"Man is like a breath; his days are like a fleeting shadow."**
>
> **Psalm 144:4**

> **"However many years a man may live, let him enjoy them all."**
>
> **Ecclesiastes 11:8**

SONS OF KORAH

Do you have a scandalous skeleton in your family closet? The Sons of Korah, the authors of Psalm 84 did. Numbers 16 recounts the story of their ancestors. They rose against the authority of Moses. They opposed him and attempted to usurp his leadership position. God declared a judgment on the families who participated in the sin. The earth opened up and swallowed them up with all their possessions. The continuing existence of this family line was a testimony to the grace of God. They rejoiced in God's forgiveness and mercy with realization that although they might never enter the Holy Of Holies of the Temple, they were grateful for the opportunity to serve the Lord God in the outer court.

Time

DAY FIVE

Time varies, but I think we would agree that we need to enjoy and make most of the time given to us. As we conclude Day Three, I would like us to read Psalm 84:1–2; 10–12. How would these verses sum up today's lesson?

_____

_____

_____

Allow these verses to become your prayer to the Lord today. Ask Him to enable you to enjoy and rejoice in each priceless moment of your life.

Today's Heart-Print
"However many years a man may live, let him enjoy them all."
(Ecclesiastes 11:8)

Lord,

_____

_____

_____

_____

_____

_____

_____

_____

END OF THE BEGINNING

For death is no more than a turning of us over from time to eternity[7]
—William Penn

Top Questions Asked by Children:

"Why?"

"Why is the sky blue?"

"Why do cats purr?"

"Why can't I go?"

Children want to know the reason for things.

We all have questions about something. We ask how, when, where, why, or who?

When will an earthquake rattle the earth?

How will I pay for my children's college tuition?

Why do I love him?

Who will take care of me when I am old?

Why does evil exist?

How and when will time end for me?

What is heaven like?

Our inquisitive minds ask questions that many times cannot be answered. But these are not new to mankind; the Bible is filled with people in search of answers. Here in Day Five we are going to research questions asked long ago by people pertaining to the subject of time.

📖 Read Proverbs 30:2–4. Write down the questions asked in these verses.

_____

_____

_____

I believe we can discover the answers to these questions asked by Agur. Note the answers to the questions found in the suggested verses.

"Who has gone up to heaven and come down?" (Read John 6:33–42; Ephesians 4:7–10)

"Who has gathered up the wind in the hollow of his hands?" (Read Luke 8:22–25)

"Who has wrapped up the waters in his cloak?" (Read Exodus 14:21–31; John 6:16–21)

"Who has established all the ends of the earth?" (Read Isaiah 45:12; Colossian 1:15–16)

"What is his name and name of his son? Tell me if you know?" (Mark 1:1; 1 John 4:15)

God the Father and His son, Jesus Christ control the wind and the waters of earth. Jesus descended to earth and ascended back into heaven. He could do this because He is God. He did it for us.

As we studied in Day One, Jesus is the Alpha and Omega, the Beginning and the End. I believe we should look to Him and His Word to answer our questions on the end of time, including our own here on earth.

📖 Read the following verses and summarize what you discern about death.

Psalm 23:4

_____

_____

_____

John 10:11–15

_____

_____

_____

My Heart's Cry:

My Good Shepherd, I have so many questions about life and eternity. Although I know I can't expect answers to all my questions, I ask for wisdom and the spirit of revelation to enhance my understanding the Bible. For within Your Word lies all I need to know this side of eternity. Thank You, Lord, for giving us Your Word.

1 Corinthians 15:55–56

_____
_____
_____

Extra Mile
JOB

We aren't the only ones who ask questions. Read Job 23:1-7; 38-42:1-6. What did Job say he would like to do? In what fashion did God answer Job? Did God ever answer His own questions to Job? What was Job's response at the end of the dialogue?

1 Corinthians 13:12

_____
_____
_____

Psalm 17:15

_____
_____
_____

Read Proverbs 11:7. What is the result for the wicked after death?

_____
_____

Read Proverbs 10:28. What is the prospect of the righteous?

_____
_____

"And I—in righteousness I will see your face; when I awake, I will be satisfied with seeing your likeness."

Psalm 17:15

How does Psalm 17:15 explain the joy and satisfaction of the righteous?

_____
_____

Write your personal thoughts concerning these verses: Proverbs 10:28, Proverbs 11:7, Psalm 17:15.

_____
_____
_____
_____

As Christians, we need not fear death. Christ, our Good Shepherd, gave His life so we might have eternal life. His death and resurrection removed the sting of death for believers. After our physical deaths, we will see and understand clearly the righteousness that Jesus bestowed upon us. Let's look at one more passage that deals with how death takes place for Christians.

Read Philippians 1:21–23.

Fill in the blanks of Philippians 1:21;

_"For to me, to live is _____ and to _____ is_
_____."_

What are your thoughts regarding the apostle Paul's statement?

_____

_____

_____

As believers in Jesus Christ as our Savior, we continue to live physically here on earth and Christ dwells *within* us. However, when we die we will be with Jesus Christ in heaven for eternity. As we study the Heart-Print of Time let's look at what awaits us in eternity—the end of the beginning.

📖 Summarize the following Scriptures:

John 14:2–3

_____

_____

_____

Revelation 21:3–5

_____

_____

_____

Revelation 22:3–5

_____

_____

_____

Ecclesiastes 3:11

_____

_____

_____

Heaven will be heavenly! No more tears, no more pain or sorrow. I don't believe it is even describable in human terms. Jesus awaits us with a home that He has prepared. Of course, the gazing into the eyes of our beloved Redeemer, Jesus, will be an unimaginable sight to behold.

📖 Please read Job 19:25–27.

🙏 Meditate on these final verses. Will you journal your own feelings on the future and spending eternity with Jesus, the Good Shepherd?

_____

_____

_____

_____

_____

_____

_____

"When the wicked die, that's it—the story's over, end of hope"

Proverbs 11:7 (The Message)

Put Yourself in Their Shoes
THE APOSTLE PAUL

Life is hard. Paul stated, *"To me to live is Christ, to die is gain."* Read 2 Corinthians 11:23-33 concerning the troubles Paul endured. Life was very difficult for Paul—no wonder he looked forward to heaven.

JOB 19:25–27

"I know that my Redeemer lives, and that in the end he will stand upon the earth. And after my skin has been destroyed, yet in my flesh I will see God; I myself will see him with my own eyes—I, and not another. How my heart yearns within me!"

Today's Heart-Print

"He has made everything beautiful in its time. He has also set eternity in the hearts of men; yet they cannot fathom what God has done from beginning to end." (Ecclesiastes 3:11)

Your Heart's Impression

Journal your thoughts about:

Your hopes and fears of the future.

_____

_____

The season of life you are currently in.

_____

_____

Spending your time wisely.

_____

_____

_____

Enjoying the priceless moments of life.

_____

_____

_____

What you expect heaven to be like for you.

_____

_____

_____

1. http://www.whatquote.com/quotes/Saint-Augustine/2544-What-then-is-time—I.htm

2. John Cook, *The Book of Positive Quotations* (New York: Grammercy Books, 193), 246.

3. http://thinkexist.com/quotation/how_we_spend_our_days_is_of_course-how_we_spend/220917.html

4. Cook, *The Book of Positive Quotations*, 216.

5. Baker, Warren D.R.E. and Eugene Carpenter, Ph.D.; eds. The Complete Word Study Dictionary Old Testament (Chattanooga, TN: AMG Publishers, 2003).

6. Ibid., 235.

7. http://www.brainyquote.com/quotes/authors/w/william_penn.html

Heart-Print for Women Only

If the time should ever come when women are not Christians and houses are not homes, then we shall have lost the chief cornerstones of which civilization rests.—Andrew Dickson White[1]

Culture influences the way we think about ourselves. Our exposures to various types of iconic women pressure us to believe we should be just like "her." Consider the wide variety of women most of us have been exposed to during our lifetimes.

- 1950s *Leave It to Beaver*: June Cleaver—The perfect wife and mother.
- 1960s *That Girl*: Ann Marie—the successful single and independent woman.
- 1970s *Wonder Woman:* Diana Prince—Beautiful and physically fit, she takes on bad guys in a bathing suit and stiletto shoes.
- 1980s *Roseanne*: Roseanne Conner—The uncouth, slovenly, and obnoxious "domestic goddess."
- 1990s *Seinfeld*: Elaine Benes—The cute, ditzy, promiscuous, and eclectic pal of Jerry Seinfeld.
- 2000s *Desperate Housewives:* Gabrielle Marques—bone thin, manic, and depressed woman with no morals.

With the role confusion we have seen throughout the years on television alone, it's no wonder most women struggle with identity issues. Who are we called to be? What is our purpose?

The good news is that God designed us. Plus, He has a perfect plan and purpose for us. In this lesson we will peruse the Book of Proverbs one final time to discover a Heart-Print for women *only*. Let's discover what identity God intends for us to claim.

With the role confusion we have seen throughout the years on television alone, it's no wonder most women struggle with identity issues.

THE WIFE FACTOR

God save us all from wives who are angels in the street, saints in the church and devil's at home.—Charles Spurgeon[2]

I grew up in a small town in northern Utah. My home would have been considered a traditional home at the time. My mother stayed home. She kept the house, cooked the meals, did the laundry, and watched after me. Once a week she would get together with her girlfriends and play bingo. As a wife, she took care of the tasks that were considered "domestic."

On the other hand, my father was a blue-collar worker on the Rio Grande Railroad. He worked hard during the day and came home expecting to be able to relax and watch TV. I don't recall my dad ever combing my hair or getting me ready for bed. He didn't do dishes, vacuum, or the laundry. It wasn't in his job description.

As a young girl, I thought my life would be very similar. I would marry, have babies, and take care of my home. Surprise! Cultural roles changed. In the eighties, we were told women could and should have it all. Society told us to be an adoring wife, the perfect mom and hold a successful career. So, I followed the cultural norm of the time, I became a working woman, a tired wife, and grouchy mom. The slow-cooking crock-pot became my best friend. Toss some food in it before work and by dinner we ate a conglomeration of meat, vegetables, and soupy sauce. (My kids still despise still pot roast.)

Thankfully, I believe women's roles are finding a balance. We realize we don't have to do and be everything to everyone. Although many women still choose to work outside the home, I believe the cultural pressure has dissipated. Many more choices are now available to women. In addition, most men help with household chores and are more willing to take care of the children's needs.

For example, both of my daughter-in-laws work and have young children. For the time being, they are privileged to work from home for their individual companies. Now some corporations provide childcare for their employees at on-site or nearby facilities. The crock-pot gets less of a work out, but is usually around the kitchen somewhere for those hectic days that still occur on a regular basis. Their husbands change the diapers, vacuum floors, and grocery shop when the need arises. It's much easier to be an adoring wife when you come home to a clean home and dinner on the table on occasion. Do you agree?

APPLY Describe your home life growing up.

_____

_____

_____

How is your role as a wife and woman different from what you experienced as a child?

_____

_____

My Heart's Cry:

Lord, I desire to be a good wife. Today as I read and study give my heart the ability to comprehend where I need to make improvements. Allow Your Holy Spirit to dig deep and root out anything that may cause damage to my husband and children. In Jesus' name, Amen.

Now let's look at how the Bible describes the role of a woman and a wife.

📖 Read Proverbs 18:22. What does this verse state?

_____

_____

_____

📖 A wife is from the Lord. I hope our husbands appreciate that fact. Read the following proverbs and jot down the good qualities and bad traits of a wife.

Proverbs 12:4

_____

_____

Proverbs 14:1

_____

_____

Proverbs 19:14

_____

_____

Do you consider yourself a godly wife? Why or why not?

_____

_____

_____

As wives, we have the ability to build up our home or tear it down with foolish behaviors. If we allow God to instill godly character in us as women, it will automatically benefit our husbands. However the reverse is true, too. If we disgrace our husbands with our words or actions, decay may creep into the marriage. We have the power to build or destroy. The Proverbs reveal a few more examples of how wives can harm their families.

📖 Summarize the following proverbs:

Proverbs 19:13b

_____

_____

Proverbs 21:9

_____

_____

Proverbs 21:19

_____

_____

> **"Better to live in a desert than with a quarrelsome and ill-tempered wife."**
>
> **Proverbs 21:19**

Proverbs 25:24

_____

_____

Extra Mile
DAVID AND MICHAL

What makes a good wife turn into a poor wife? Read the following Scripture passages to discover how the relationship changed between David and Michal.

- I Samuel 18:20, 27
- I Samuel 19:11–17
- I Samuel 25:39–44
- 2 Samuel 3:13–16
- 2 Samuel 6:16–23

List the events in Michal's life. How did her feelings change toward David? Why? In your opinion, what could Michal have done to prevent her bitterness (see Hebrews 12:14–15)?

What do you tend to grumble about the most with your husband and children? Is your grumbling an annoyance to your family? Do they wish they lived in the desert?

According to Proverbs 19:13, a whining, grumbling woman is like constant dripping—I liken this to the annoyance of a leaky faucet. Today let's keep in mind the monotonous sound of a dripping faucet or the annoyance of a constantly running toilet and then think of how our incessant grumbling can have a similar effect on our families. Let's ask God to help make us more conscious of how negative we can sound when we grumble. Do you think our spouses will be pleasantly surprised when we grumble less and encourage more?

📖 Unfortunately, there are causes for unhappy women in the world. Read Proverbs 30:21–23 and note the third cause that can make the earth tremble.

_____

_____

According to Proverbs 30:21–23, an unloved wife makes the earth tremble. Are you familiar with this quote, "Heaven has no rage like love to hatred turned, nor hell a fury like a woman scorned." If a woman feels unloved, she will behave unlovely. Without using names, do you know any women who have felt scorned by a man? What was her reaction?

_____

_____

_____

_____

_____

_____

OK, just for a moment let's pick on the men. What type of trouble can men bring to a marriage?

Proverbs 5:15–20

_____

_____

Proverbs 11:29

_____

_____

Ecclesiastes 10:18

_____

_____

Proverbs 27:8

_____

_____

_____

A man, as well as a woman, can bring trouble into a home. The phrase, *"drink from your own cisterns,"* refers to men remaining faithful to the wives of their youth. Men who stray from faithfulness in marriage will destroy their homes. Unfaithfulness can include watching pornography, reckless flirting, adultery, mental or physical abuse. If your husband (or yourself) is involved in any of these behaviors, please seek out professional marriage counseling.

📖 All right, let's get back to us. Let's find out what will make us better wives. What does Proverbs 11:16 state about a good wife?

_____

_____

🙏 Today as we close in prayer, let's ask the Lord to aid us in learning to be prudent and gracious wives. We want to be considered good wives by our husbands, but more importantly by God.

Today's Heart Print
"He who finds a wife finds what is good and receives favor from the Lord."
(Proverbs 18:22)

Lord,

_____

_____

_____

_____

_____

_____

_____

MEAN GIRLS

A man without religion is to be pitied, but a Godless woman is a horror above all things.—Augusta Jane Evans[4]

Mean Girls. Do you remember the ones from seventh and eighth grade? I can still visualize one and her perky turned-up nose and tilt of her head. It seems most women cannot go through life without female conflict of one sort or another.

Word Study
PRUDENT

The term "prudent" brings to mind someone who is tight fisted with money. But in Proverbs 19:14, the Hebrew equivalent of this word expands on this thought. Prudent comes from the Hebrew word, sakal. This word entails the following ideas: to be circumspect, be prudent, to teach, to have wisdom, skill, or expertise, to be intelligent, to consider; to have understanding, insight, or intellectual comprehension, to be upright and pious.[3]

For Women Only

DAY TWO

My Heart's Cry:

Father, I do not want to be considered a godless woman. Although, society states it is all right to trample on others, give me a heart of love. Lord, let my mouth and actions model godliness to others. In Your Son's name, Amen.

In February 2002, *The New York Times Magazine* article "Girls Just Want To Be Mean and the New Movement to Tame Them" brought the topic of mean girls to the water cooler discussions at the office. Recent books and movies portray the phenomenon of contemptible female behavior. Mean girls have been around a long time. In the 1800's, Henry Wadsworth Longfellow wrote the familiar nursery rhyme that sums up such women.

> *There was a little girl,*
> *Who had a little curl,*
> *Right in the middle of her forehead.*
> *When she was good,*
> *She was very good indeed,*
> *But when she was bad she was horrid.*

Today we are going to study a woman who was horrid—Jezebel. She lived in ancient Israel, but her story lives on. There will be quite a bit of reading in the beginning of this lesson from 1 and 2 Kings, and then we'll proceed to see how the Proverbs apply to a mean girl, Jezebel.

📖 Please read 1 Kings 16:29–31; 18:3–4, 13–14; 19:1–2; 21:1–16 and 2 Kings 9:22, 30–33.

Describe the attitude and actions of Jezebel.

_____

_____

_____

_____

In the first verse we read about King Ahab and his sin with the added note of, *"but he also married Jezebel."* Obviously she was a woman with a horrid reputation long before Ahab married her. With the power she obtained from becoming queen, she ruled from behind the throne. She killed God's prophets, murdered Naboth for his vineyard, and she sought to execute Elijah, the prophet. We also know according to 2 Kings 9:22 that Jezebel practiced idolatry and witchcraft in abundance. As the saying goes, she had quite a reputation for evil, wouldn't you say?

📖 Let's read a few proverbs and determine how they might or might not apply to Jezebel. Note the evil traits of Jezebel. Then note the godly traits she lacked.

Proverbs 5:21–23

_____

_____

Proverbs 15:16

_____

_____

Proverbs 19:10

_____

_____

Proverbs 19:12

_____

_____

Proverbs 27:15–16

_____

_____

Proverbs 28:12

_____

_____

Proverbs 28:15

_____

_____

How does Proverbs 21:10 relate to Jezebel and Naboth?

_____

_____

How does Proverbs 21:12 apply to God and Jezebel?

_____

_____

> **"The Righteous One takes note of the house of the wicked and brings the wicked to ruin."**
>
> **Proverbs 21:12**

Read Roman 1:29–31. Circle each sin mentioned that Jezebel committed.

> _"They have become filled with every kind of wickedness, evil, greed and depravity. They are full of envy, murder, strife, deceit and malice. They are gossips, slanderers, God-haters, insolent, arrogant and boastful; they invent ways of doing evil; they disobey their parents; they are senseless, faithless, heartless, ruthless."_ (Romans 1:29–31)

Jezebel was filled with every kind of wickedness, evil greed, and depravity. We read of murder, strife, deceit, and malice. She hated God. Her insolent arrogant behavior eventually cost her very life.

📖 Read Galatians 6:7 and Ecclesiastes 12:13–14. Summarize how these two verses compare with the death of Jezebel.

_____

_____

God will not be mocked. He will bring into judgment every deed—good and bad. Anything that Jezebel thought she was hiding was in clear view to God's eyes. In His righteousness, He brought an end to the evil of Jezebel.

📖 Read what the mother of King Lemuel advised in Proverbs 31:1–3. How would you apply this to Jezebel and Ahab?

_____

_____

> **"For God will bring every deed into judgment, including every hidden thing, whether it is good or evil."**
>
> **Ecclesiastes 12:14**

It's too bad that Ahab didn't hear this proverb and recognize the wisdom in it. Ahab allowed Jezebel to influence him in many areas. He became weak as she became stronger.

Let's take a moment to consider our own situations. Can you share a time when you encountered a mean female?

_____

_____

_____

I remember a time when two of my best friends tried to hide from me at school. I spotted them giggling and laughing as they ran off. Another time, a girl I didn't even know grabbed my head under her harm and began to pound on me. I was young when these events occurred, but they are still fresh in my memory.

Even as an adult, I have experienced mean women. I served as a Women's ministries director for four years. After a tortuous day, I would come home and turn my back toward my husband and half-jokingly say, "Honey, will you please pull the knives out of my back?" Women can be brutal to each other.

📖 Scripture suggests we train each other in godly behaviors. Read Titus 2:3-5 and then list what we can learn from each other as women.

_____

_____

_____

_____

Many devout women mentored me on how to be a godly woman. They taught me what is good and acceptable behavior according to the Word of God. They aided me in learning self-control and kindness. They instructed me on how to love my husband and my children. And most important, they taught me to honor Christ in all areas of my womanhood.

Who discipled you in your walk as a woman of God?

_____

_____

Do you have a friend whom you are mentoring?

_____

_____

How does teaching another woman aid us in our own behaviors?

_____

_____

Day Two gave us much to contemplate. Let's ask Christ to dig deep in our hearts to bring to light the residual meanness that remains. Let's ask Him to make us aware of any sinful behavior that distorts a godly personality. Finally, if you know a "Jezebel" take a few minutes to pray for her.

My Jesus,

_____

_____

_____

_____

_____

_____

_____

_____

MIRROR, MIRROR ON THE WALL

Mirror, mirror, on the wall, who in this land is fairest of all?
—Snow White's Stepmother

Fairy tales usually center on the beauty of the heroine in the tale. Think for a moment: *Beauty and the Beast*, *Snow White*, *Sleeping Beauty*, *Cinderella*, and *Rapunzel*. The beauty possessed by the heroines in each of these tales charts the plot for the rest of the story.

In modern culture we not only deal with the written fairy tales, we see airbrushed models staring out at us from magazine covers in the grocery checkout line. Television and movies espouse and celebrate beautiful women who have designer clothes, make-up artists, and traveling hairdressers.

And then, the greatest fairy tale of all—Barbie. By now, most of us have heard that if we looked like Barbie this would be our body proportions: Bust 39 inches, waist 18 inches, hips 32 inches, all this on a 5'9" frame weighing approximately 110 pounds standing on size 3 feet.[5]

Physical appearance plays a major role in most women's day-to-day contentment. We worry about our weight. I love the commercial that shows women with a scale chained to their ankle. As they go through their daily activities, the old Willie Nelson song, "You Were Always on My Mind," plays softly in the background. We rush out to buy the latest wrinkle cream. We watch reality television that shows plastic surgery makeovers and wonder would it help us?

I am angry as I write this. Angry at a culture that dictates a woman's beauty. I am furious that my friend's daughter is in a rehabilitation facility for an eating disorder. Livid at myself, for the money I have spent on products that promise me a youthful appearance. I look older today than I did yesterday. So where does it end?

My Heart's Cry:

Father, I know that You created me according to Your perfect design. But I admit that when I gaze in the mirror there are parts of me I don't like. Help me to realize that I am beautiful to You. Help me stop comparing myself to other women.

In Day Three we will spend our time together looking at what God says about a woman's physical beauty. Let's see if we can ascertain the contentment God intended for us when it comes to our physical bodies.

 Place an X on the line below to indicate what you see when you study yourself in the mirror.

← →

Mirror Cracks   A few flaws   Average   Almost perfection   I am Barbie!

What is your best physical feature?

_____

_____

What would you like to change if you could?

_____

_____

For most of us, we are average in appearance. We all have a few flaws and some beautiful features. I love my eyes but hate my thighs. But enough about ourselves, let's see what God has to say about beauty and women.

📖 Read Proverbs 31:30.

_____

_____

If according to this proverb beauty is fleeting, in your opinion why do we chase after it so diligently?

I think it all goes back to Barbie, Hollywood, and fairy tales. We buy into the lies they promote instead of believing God. First, we need to change our thought patterns of how we perceive beauty. Please read Romans 12:2 and then fill in the following blanks.

"Do not _____ any longer to the pattern of this world, but be _____ by the _____ of your _____."

As we read the following Scriptures, ask God to help you see the truth of His words to us. Ask Him to help you conform not to the world's standards of physical loveliness, but to transform your mind to help you appreciate and love yourself.

📖 Please read Psalm 139:13-14. What do these verses mean to you?

_____

_____

_____

_____

According to this verse, the psalmist states that God shaped and knit him together. The Bible gives other descriptions of God's intimate detail in our formation. Please read Psalm 119:73 and Psalm 139:16. What additional information do these verses add to your understanding of your physical body?

"Charm is deceptive, and beauty is fleeting; but a woman who fears the Lord is to be praised."

Proverbs 31:30

FEARFULLY AND WONDERFULLY MADE

"For you created my inmost being; you knit me together in my mother's womb. I praise you because I am fearfully and wonderfully made; your works are wonderful, I know that full well." (Psalm 139:13–14)

God's hands wove us in the womb to His standard of individual perfection. We are fearfully and wonderfully made! And He wants us to find love and contentment with our bodies. Please read Mark 12:28-31. Jot down the second greatest commandment.

_____

Underline "*as yourself*" in the commandment you wrote above. Jesus expects us to love others, but He also expects that we love ourselves, too.

Do you recall Leah and Rachel from our lesson on contentment in Week 3? We're going to take a quick look at them again.

📖 Read Genesis 29:16-18; 30-32.

_____

_____

_____

Describe their physical attributes.

Leah

_____

_____

_____

Rachel

_____

_____

_____

📖 Read Proverbs 14:30. Write down the phrase in this proverb that would apply to Leah?

_____

_____

_____

📖 Read Proverbs 30:15-16. Dissatisfaction comes from a variety of sources, but what phrase of this proverbs would apply to Rachel?

_____

_____

_____

We have already learned that Leah and Rachel didn't love each other, but do you think they loved themselves? I don't believe they did. Leah didn't like her looks. Beautiful Rachel felt unworthy because of a barren womb. Let's speculate for a moment. What do you think could have happened between these two sisters if they had accepted how God had formed them in the womb?

> "Your eyes saw my unformed body. All the days ordained for me were written in your book before one of them came to be."
>
> **Psalm 139:16**

_____
_____
_____

 Maybe they could have rejoiced in the blessings of each other. I don't know, but I think they would have been happier with themselves and each other. In Day Two we studied about mean women. How often do you think envying the beauty of other women influences our behavior?

_____
_____
_____

When have you been envious of another girl's beauty?

_____
_____
_____

Did you feel that envy was "rotting your bones?"

_____
_____

Extra Mile
ESTHER

Want to find out about true beauty? Read the Book of Esther. Contemplate the following verses and then answer the questions.

- Esther 2:15–16: Why did Esther decide to only take Hegai with her?

- Esther 4:12–14: What argument did Mordecai use to change Esther's mind?

- Esther 4:15–16: How do you suppose Esther's fast strengthened her resolve?

- Can you describe Esther's beauty from God's perspective?

Although we rot away longing to be more attractive, physical beauty doesn't impress God. Isaiah 53:2, although prophesied hundreds of years before Jesus' birth, gives us a clue at how the world viewed the physical attractiveness of Jesus, our Lord: *"He grew up before him like a tender shoot, and like a root out of dry ground. He had no beauty or majesty to attract us to him, nothing in his appearance that we should desire him"* (Isaiah 53:2).

The world couldn't see the beauty of Christ. His beauty came from the inside. I believe that is the type of beauty that we should desire to have. Not only will it please our Creator, but also it will blossom into contentment within us.

📖 Please read 1 Peter 3:3-4.

Now please understand this verse doesn't say we shouldn't wear jewelry, color our hair, or purchase attractive clothes. It does say that our beauty shouldn't come from these temporary items, but we should glow with beauty from within. *The Bible Knowledge Commentary* explains it as,

> A woman who wins this kind of victory has a winsome loveliness that comes not from outward adornment but from her inner self, the unfading beauty of a gentle and quiet spirit. This adornment of the spirit is of great worth in God's sight. While the world prizes costly clothing and gold jewelry, a woman with a gentle and quiet spirit is precious to God. Peter did not state that women should not wear jewelry and nice clothes, but that Christian wives should not think of outer attire as the source of genuine beauty.[6]

How would this thought apply to Proverbs 11:22?

_____
_____

We can adorn ourselves with make-up, color our hair, elect to have plastic surgery, or wear the finest jewelry, but if we are ugly on the inside, it will show upon the exterior. Proverbs 27:19 aptly relates this truth.

In the margin, read Proverbs 27:19.

 So are you beautiful within? Journal your thoughts to God describing your physical body. Tell Him about your dislikes, and then pray that you will not continue to compare yourself to Barbie or airbrushed models. Praise Him that you are wonderfully made by His hands. Ask Him to help you love yourself and to become a gentle, kindhearted woman.

Today's Heart-Print
"Charm is deceptive, and beauty is fleeting; but a woman who fears the Lord is to be praised." (Proverbs 31:30)

Father,

_____

_____

_____

_____

_____

_____

_____

_____

_____

"Just as water mirrors your face, so your face mirrors your heart."

Proverbs 27:19 (The Message)

For Women Only

DAY FOUR

BEHIND CLOSED DOORS

Let the wife make the husband glad to come home, and let him make her sorry to see him leave.—Martin Luther[7]

America experienced the sexual revolution during the 1960s. For women, *Cosmopolitan Magazine,* now known as *"Cosmo"* remodeled how they understood their sexuality. *Cosmo* issued romance advice and sex tips. It promoted sex outside of the boundaries of marriage. The monthly publication questioned Christian morality. It encouraged women to experiment sexually, to be free, and choose your partner with abandonment. Suddenly, it seemed the destiny of a women's happiness hinged on one thing—sex.

Its chief editor, Helen Gurley Brown, followed the popularity of *Cosmo* with a bestselling book titled, *Having It All.* She wrote, "Don't assume just because you're having sex with a man that you have to (1) fall in love with him; (2) get into a big emotional dither; (3) marry him!"[8] Poor advice, Ms. Brown!

God created sexual intimacy as a gift inside the confines of marriage. He wants us to enjoy sex behind closed doors with our husbands. He does not

My Heart's Cry:

Father, today help me to realize the importance of physical love in marriage. I thank You for the gift of my sexuality. Teach me to use this gift in a godly manner and way that You divinely intended.

Put Yourself in Their Shoes
JOSEPH

All through the Bible, we find men and women who struggle with the temptation of sexual sin. Read Genesis 39:2–12 and the account of Joseph literally running from temptation! Compare Proverbs 23:26–28 to Potiphar's wife. How does 1 Corinthians 10:13 apply to Joseph and his reaction? What would you have done in Joseph's situation?

condone sex outside of marriage. Today we will counter *Cosmo* with God's Word. As we read the Proverbs for today's lesson, keep in mind that they were written to a young man. However, the same advice also applies to women.

📖 Read Proverbs 6:23-29. Paraphrase verse 23.

_____

_____

Note the characteristics of how an immoral person entices.

Verse 24

_____

_____

Verse 25

_____

_____

What warning is given in Verse 26?

_____

_____

Condense verses 27-29 into one sentence.

_____

_____

These verses assert that good looks, a smooth tongue, bedroom eyes, and plain human lust can entice us into situations where we get burned. Let's dissect another passage concerning sexual temptation. As you read, place yourself in the shoes of the son listening to his father.

📖 Read Proverbs 7:4-27.

In this passage, the father explains the importance of maintaining sexual purity. Author Max Anders explains, "He dramatizes the story of seduction, taking his son through a verbal role-playing scenario to prepare him for the real thing, explaining the specific details as a way to prepare his son to deal with such situations."[9] As Christian women, we must be aware of our sexual influence on men.

Reread Verse 10. How do you think the way we dress affect men?

_____

_____

📖 Our attire holds the power to tempt men because they are more visually stimulated. The apostle Paul gave instruction on how women should dress. Read 1 Timothy 2:9-10.

In your opinion, what fashion styles in our culture would be considered indecent or inappropriate?

_____

_____

Now don't get hung-up on whether we should braid our hair or wear gold jewelry and expensive clothes. The point Paul makes is that we need to dress with modesty. That doesn't mean we can't look beautiful in that new cashmere sweater, but it denotes we should not look overtly sexy either.

Read Romans 13:13-14. How is this verse similar to Proverbs 7:4-27 and 1 Timothy 2:9-10?

_____

_____

_____

The Proverbs state emphatically that we must be on our guard against any type of sexual temptation outside of marriage. This includes our behavior in how we dress and act to influence men. In addition, it warns us to lookout for times when we might be tempted to sin sexually. Romans 13:14 gives us the unsurpassed answer to all sexual seduction, *"Clothe yourself with the Lord Jesus Christ and do not think about how to gratify the desires of the sinful nature."* Quite a bit different from the advice you get from *Cosmo,* isn't it?

Many of us have failed miserably in this area of sexual temptation. Shame sits on our shoulders, and shadows our walk with Jesus. But God is in the business of mercy and forgiveness.

Read John 8:1-11. Write down what Jesus said and did.

_____

_____

_____

_____

OK, so what about making love with our husbands? Let's read the following verses to pinpoint what God has to say about our love life.

Read the following verses and summarize their instructions to husbands and wives.

Genesis 1:27-28; 2:24-25

_____

_____

_____

Proverbs 5:18-19

_____

_____

_____

1 Corinthians 7:1-5

_____

_____

_____

"Rather, clothe yourselves with the Lord Jesus Christ, and do not think about how to gratify the desires of the sinful nature."

Romans 13:14

" 'Then neither do I condemn you' Jesus declared. 'Go now and leave your life of sin.' "

John 8:11

God intends for intimate lovemaking between a husband and wife to be fulfilling emotionally and physically. He wants marital love to last a lifetime, not just a whimsy that we grow tired of in a few months. He designed sex to be a gift in marriage, a secret pleasure between a man and a woman who have taken vows of faithfulness to each other. So regardless of what *Cosmo* touts, we know the truth about sexual freedom behind closed doors with our spouses—thanks to those explicit Proverbs.

Today's Heart-Print

"May your fountain be blessed, and may you rejoice in the wife of your youth. A loving doe, a graceful deer—may her breasts satisfy you always, may you ever be captivated by her love." (Proverbs 5:18-19)

 Share your thoughts on sexual temptation, purity, and sexual intimacy with your heavenly Father. He desires for you to sit by His knee and listen closely to His instruction on this matter.

Heavenly Father,

_____

_____

_____

_____

_____

_____

_____

_____

THE TOTAL WOMAN

Earth's noblest thing, a Woman perfected.—James Russell Lowell[10]

"You look tired," my girlfriend states. I tingle with pride. I wear my exhaustion as a badge of honor. It's an unfortunate fact that many women in America place an emotional value on the commodity of exhaustion.

Even my husband has noticed that women often comment on how tired we seem to look to each other. He thinks it sounds like we are attempting to compliment each other. He once told me, "I would be insulted if a guy ever said that to me."

Granted moms have a lot to do, and I have never been a high-energy gal. My energy and stamina ebb on the low side. It seems when God created me, He wired me tired. God created each of us with our own energy levels. Mine happens to be low wattage.

However, sometimes envy floats to the surface. I compare myself to women who bounce around full of exuberant energy, completing every task set before them. Their endless supply of enthusiasm saps my vitality. I covet their high-energy personalities. Their houses resemble model homes. The birthday parties they give their children come complete with clowns, piñatas, and a faultless homemade cake. Their hair flips just right. Manicured nails match ten perfect toes. The ironed creases in their jeans accentuate the spotless white blouse. They appear to be the living example of the woman found in Proverbs 31.

In the 1970's Marabel Morgan wrote the bestseller, *The Total Woman*. It stressed having the home tidy, taking care of yourself physically, respecting your husband and of course, being a sex kitten for him. She taught seminars and gave homework. One assignment instructed the wife to thrill her husband at the front door. She wrote, "A frilly new nighty and heels will probably do the trick as starter. Variety is the spice of life."[11] One of her students reported on humorous result of her assignment that she "dressed a la gypsy with beads, bangles, and bare skin," greeted her equally-surprised water meter reader—but later she thrilled her husband.[12] Another woman took the assignment to heart by dressing herself in just saran wrap with a big red bow.[13] However, what Marabel's book portrayed was an ideal even Barbie couldn't compete with. The same could be said about The Proverbs 31 woman—perfection and grace unattainable.

Is it possible to do it all? Of course not. But in this final lesson, we examine the Proverbs 31 woman. Although we cannot attain perfection this side of heaven, we can be godly women of excellence in all areas of lives—when we allow Christ to do in us and through what He alone can do.

📖 Please read Proverbs 31:10-31.

This passage differs from any other part of the Book of Proverbs. These verses appear in a poetic format in the form of an acrostic. In other words, each successive line of these verses begins with the next letter of the Hebrew alphabet. The first word in verse 10 starts with the Hebrew equivalent of the letter "A," verse 11 with "B," and so on all the way to verse 31, which begins with the Hebrew equivalent of the letter "Z." This is a description of a good wife from A to Z! The acrostic form was typically used as an aid toward memorization.

Honestly, how do you feel about such a woman? Isn't she too good to be true? Well, she is to me. I thought you might find it interesting only one actual woman in the entire Bible is said to be "noble."

📖 Read Ruth 3:1–11. How did Boaz describe Ruth?

_____

_____

_____

Match the following proverbs with the correct attribute found in the Proverbs 31 woman.

Proverbs 11:16	Proverbs 31:26—She speaks with wisdom
Proverbs 12:4	Proverbs 31:31b—Let her works bring her praise
Proverbs 15:7	Proverbs 31:11—Husband has confidence in her
Proverbs 17:6	Proverbs 31:28—Her children praise her

📖 Compare Proverbs 31:10 with Proverbs 8:11. What did you discover?

My Heart's Cry:

Lord, I am not perfect. As I have studied these past ten weeks, I recognize many flaws within myself. Remind me that everyday is a new day to aspire toward making myself into the total woman that You purposed for me when You formed me in the womb. In Your name, Amen.

"Many women do noble things, but you surpass them all."

Proverbs 31:29

Word Study
NOBLE

The term noble in Proverbs 31:10, (or virtuous in the King James Version) derives from the Hebrew word, hayil. Hayil pertains to strength, wealth, and is often associated with army strength. It conveys the basic idea of strength and influence. God is often seen in Scripture as the supplier of this strength.[14]

"A wife of noble character who can find? She is worth far more than rubies."

Proverbs 31:10

The Proverbs 31 woman is as valuable as wisdom. She is priceless. As we examine the Proverbs 31 woman, think back through our ten weeks of study on the Book of Proverbs. Below is the list of topics we have covered. Write out the corresponding verse of the Proverbs 31 woman that exemplifies the lesson.

Heart-Print of Wisdom (Proverbs 31:30b)

_____

_____

Heart-Print of Trust (Proverbs 31:25b)

_____

_____

Heart-Print of Contentment (Proverbs 31:27)

_____

_____

Heart-Print of Friendship (Proverbs 31:20)

_____

_____

Heart-Print of Emotions (Proverbs 31:25a)

_____

_____

Heart-Print of Motherhood (Proverbs 31:28)

_____

_____

Heart-Print of Conversation (Proverbs 31:26)

_____

_____

Heart-Print of Finances (Proverbs 31:16)

_____

_____

Heart-Print of Time (Proverbs 31:27)

_____

_____

Heart-Print for Women Only (Proverbs 31:11-12)

_____

_____

We began this week with an overview of some of the cultural influences that affect our view on how we should act as women. We close with the scriptural ideal of a woman. In the Proverbs 31 woman we discover a woman with faith, skill, ingenuity, community involvement, and recognition for her achievements as a wife and mother. She is the total woman.

Well, we did it. We journeyed though the Book of Proverbs together. We learned wisdom, desired contentment, discussed friendship, deciphered our emotions, and learned to be women of virtue. I think it would be fitting to close with a few final words of Solomon in Ecclesiastes 12:13.

Today's Heart-Print
"Now all has been heard; here is the conclusion of the matter: Fear God and keep his commandments, for this is the whole duty of man."
(Ecclesiastes 12:13)

Your Heart's Impression

Journal your thoughts about:

Excelling as a wife:

_____

_____

_____

_____

_____

Women who purposely hurt others.

_____

_____

_____

_____

_____

What you learned about sexual intimacy.

_____

_____

_____

_____

_____

How will you begin to become more like the Proverbs 31 woman?

_____

_____

_____

_____

_____

"For wisdom is more precious than rubies, and nothing you desire can compare with her."

Proverbs 8:11

Extra Mile
RUTH

Ruth was a noble woman. If you would like to know more about why she was characterized as such, read the Book of Ruth in the Bible. Pay special attention to her behavior with Naomi, her mother-in-law. Note how diligent she worked to provide for Naomi and herself. How did she behave with Boaz? How did God reward her virtuous spirit?

Tell the Lord God what is in your heart after this study on the Proverbs.

Lord God,

_____

_____

_____

_____

_____

_____

_____

_____

_____

1. Frank S. Mead, *12,000 Religious Quotations* (Grand Rapids, MI: Baker Book House, 1989). 472

2. Ibid., 469

3. http://www.time.com/time/magazine/article/0,9171,947281-3,00.html

4. Ibid., 470.

5. Margo Maine, *Body Wars: An Activist's Guide* (Carlsbad, CA, 2000,) 210

6. *Bible Knowledge Commentary*. Underlying source materials. c 1983, by Scripture Press Publications, Inc. Licensed by Victor Books. Database c1997 NavPress Software.

7. http://www.brainyquote.com/quotes/authors/m/martin_luther.html

8. Helen Gurley Brown, *Having It All* (New York: Simon and Schuster, 1982), 222.

9. Max Anders, *Holman Old Testament Commentary-Proverbs* (Nashville, TN. Holman Reference, 2005), 60.

10. http://www.bartleby.com/100/501.html

11. Marabel Morgan, *The Total Woman* (Old Tappan, NJ: Fleming H. Revell Company, 1973), 127.

12. Ibid., 99.

13. Ibid.

14. Warren Baker, D.R.E. and Eugene Carpenter, Ph.D.; eds. *The Complete WordStudy Dictionary Old Testament* (Chattanooga, TN: AMG Publishers, 2003).

Made in the USA
Middletown, DE
20 February 2022